TASTES
OF AFRICA

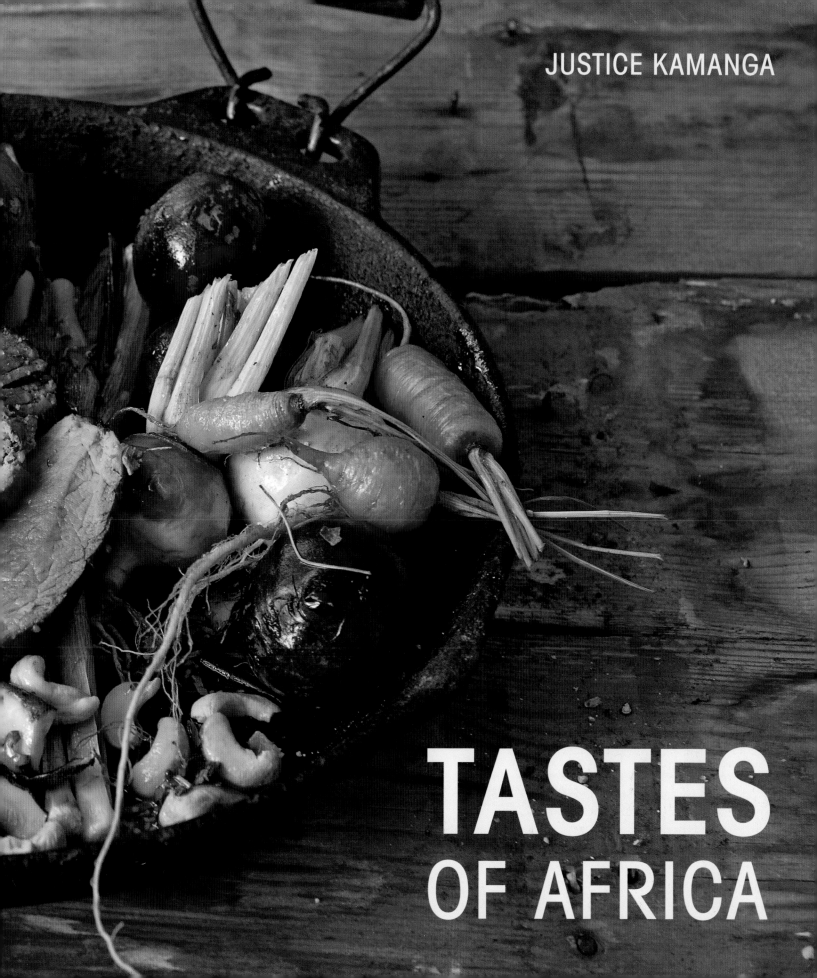

JUSTICE KAMANGA

TASTES
OF AFRICA

ACKNOWLEDGEMENTS

I would like to thank all those people who worked so hard to make this exciting and amazing book possible. It has been a dream come true for me and what my eyes have seen, my heart cannot believe. It has been a pleasure working with all of you: Linda, Beverley and Cecilia at Random House Struik, as well as photographer Ryno, and Brita and Jen.

I would also like to thank my special family for all their love and support: Roseleena, Kevisto, Isaack, Alucia, Leeare, Johnson, Justice jnr, Devison and Wesley.

Furthermore, I would like to thank my friends Wade, Tanith, Gavin, Lynne and Louise for everything they have done.

I hope you enjoy cooking these recipes as much as I have.

JUSTICE KAMANGA

The publishers would like to thank the following suppliers for their generous loan of props: Mnandi Textiles, Moroccan Warehouse, Out of this World, and Heartworks.

Published in 2010 by Struik Lifestyle
(an imprint of Random House Struik (Pty) Ltd)
Company Reg. No. 1966/003153/07
80 McKenzie Street, Cape Town, 8001
PO Box 1144, Cape Town, 8000, South Africa

PUBLISHER: Linda de Villiers
EDITOR: Cecilia Barfield
DESIGNER: Beverley Dodd
INTRODUCTION TEXT: Gavin Barfield
BACKGROUND RESEARCH: Lynne Harris
PHOTOGRAPHER: Ryno
STYLIST: Brita du Plessis
FOOD PREPARATION: Jen du Plessis
PROOFREADER AND INDEXER: Joy Clack
REPRODUCTION: Hirt & Carter Cape (Pty) Ltd
PRINTING AND BINDING: Tien Wah Press, Singapore

ISBN 978-1-77007-802-4

www.imagesofafrica.co.za
IMAGES OF AFRICA
PHOTO LIBRARY
Over 40 000 unique African images available to purchase from our image bank at **www.imagesofafrica.co.za**

CONTENTS

INTRODUCTION

INTRODUCTION

No matter how up-to-date, no book on African food can ever be complete. Just as the sprawling continent is itself a work in progress, so too is its cuisine in a process of flux and evolution.

The second-largest land mass on earth and home to hundreds of tribes, ethnic and social groups, Africa's diversity is reflected in its cuisine; in the use of inexpensive, basic, locally-available ingredients, as well as in the widely-differing cooking techniques and styles of preparation. Given the sheer size of the continent, the current vogue for African food means that no dish can ever be generic.

Common to many parts of the continent are meals with little meat, plenty of whole grains and beans, and fresh fruits and vegetables. In an increasingly health-conscious society, African cuisine may well become the new healthy way of cooking.

African cooking varies widely from one part of the continent to another. North, Southern, Central, East and West Africa all have their trademark dishes. This is fusion food — easily-prepared, readily-available foods that people eat now, subtly influenced by traditional African dishes. In this book you will realise how easily you can have an authentic, African-themed dinner party at home, using modern foods we eat every day, but given an easy and intriguing African slant.

While there have been many books dealing with the traditional cuisine of individual African countries, often following the fickle whims of culinary fashion, in bringing you this book Justice Kamanga reaches beyond the single-country approach to the broad essence of African cooking and takes you on a beguiling epicurean journey through the continent to the soul of its cuisine.

Just as Africa is often an enigma to the traveller, so its cuisine — paradoxically, perhaps — is deceptively simple, yet at the same time complex and unknowable in the antiquity of its ingredients, origins and preparation methods that have remained unchanged for more than a thousand years.

The tastes and flavours of Africa evoke the continent itself, relatively unknown to those who haven't visited it, or who have only done so on a hectic in-and-out business or holiday trip that never leaves the time to dig beneath the *ersatz* safari ethos to the roots of its culture and traditions.

You will discover the origins of many favourite dishes, united both by a disarming honesty and ease of preparation, and find that each fascinating flavour and intriguing new texture comes subtly through the taste of the whole, from the most caustic of curries to soothing cucumber- and yoghurt-based antidotes designed to put out the fire!

Rural sea and lakeshore folk in Africa, accustomed to eating some fairly alarming-looking things from time to time, drew the line at having a beady eye ogling them from the aromatic, saffron-hued depths of their soup. When the fishermen returned from their labours at the end of the day, locals waiting on the shore to buy their catch usually asked for the heads to be taken off. This left the vendors with a cargo of fish-heads looking up at them accusingly from the bottom of the boat. Since this is a practical land where nothing is wasted, the heads ended up in the soup, although they are always removed before serving. A few imaginative, locally-available bits of this and that were added to the fish-heads simmering in the communal stockpot, and the eventual result was a piscatorial *potage* of majestic quality. Traditionally, when available, shellfish also found their way into the soup pot, and there's a sublime crayfish soup included with the recipes that's ideal for serving as a starter before a main meat or curry dish.

A quick word on the subject of fish, though — to support conservation initiatives, before buying any fish or seafood, it is always best to check that what you're buying is on the approved 'green' list (best choice), or at least on the 'orange' list (caution) of SASSI (the Southern African Sustainable Seafood Initiative — see http://www.wwfsassi.co.za).

Central Africa, the region whose cuisine has perhaps been least influenced by the outside world, stretches from the Tibetsi mountains in the north to the basin of the Congo River, the second-largest river in Africa. Apart from the cassava, peanut and chilli-pepper plants, which arrived there via the slave trade in the early 1500s, historically the relatively inaccessible region's cooking has resisted outside influences. Like other parts of Africa, however, the cuisine of Central Africa still relies heavily on dishes containing cassava or plantains.

The determinedly stodgy *fufu,* for example, is probably the best-known Central African staple, particularly in Cameroon, where it is sometimes called *Couscous de Cameroon* (although it bears no resemblance at all to the exalted Moroccan product of the same name). Similar to *pap* in South Africa, *sadza* in Zimbabwe and *ugali* in Kenya, it's a sort of stiff porridge, made out of starchy root vegetables. Normally beaten with a mortar and pestle until the desired consistency is reached, *fufu* is often eaten with okra, dried fish or tomato, and goes well with palm-nut or groundnut (peanut) soup. Central African countries are hot on their soups; among the best are those made with either smoked or unsmoked meat or fish. The eater breaks off a piece of *fufu* and makes a depression or an indentation in it with his or her thumb. A little of the soup is scooped up, and the *fufu* folded over the soup into a crude ball, which is then eaten.

*Fufu-*like starchy foods accompany grilled meat and sauces. A variety of local ingredients is used, and one particular favourite is *bambara,* a porridge of rice, peanut butter and sugar. Beef and chicken are much-loved meat dishes, but the locals in that part of the world are into bush meat in a big way — and it is not unusual to find dishes containing monkey, crocodile, warthog and antelope on the menu.

Although fishing is carried on extensively in the region's numerous rivers, and people are hungry, the parlous state of the economies of many central African countries is such that whatever is caught is almost always bartered or sold from the fishermen's boats to Democratic Republic of the Congo buyers on that side of the Ubangi River before the boat even hits land for the first time.

In many parts of East Africa, on the other hand, cattle, sheep and goats are not generally seen as food, but are viewed instead as a form of currency and an indicator of wealth. East African cooking varies sharply from area to area. In the inland savannah area, for example, meat products are generally absent from the diets of the cattle-keeping population. Particularly at the coast, the influence of Arabic invaders around one thousand years ago and subsequent Portuguese settlers brought about changes in the cuisine with cinnamon, cloves, costly saffron and other spices coming to the forefront of the area's cooking, as well as a preference for spiced steamed rice and pomegranate juice. A later wave of Portuguese arrivals brought exotic marinades and a move towards stewing and roasting, rather than grilling. The British and Indians followed centuries afterwards, and while the Indians bequeathed subtle and complex curries and delicacies such as chapattis, lentils and pickles, quite what the UK contributed is open to conjecture!

Oysters, which feature very little in African cooking, became a favourite of Kenyan colonial society when an old recipe, included in this book, found its way to British expatriates in that country via the Kenyan port of Mombasa on the east coast. Plump, subtle and succulent, Kenyan oysters are still prized today.

As far as North Africa is concerned, Morocco is one of the few countries in Africa that's self-sufficient from a food point of view. Larger than California, the nomads and Berbers who crossed it two thousand and more years ago used readily-available local ingredients such as figs, olives and dates to prepare traditional lamb, goat and poultry stews. Generally enjoyed with the stews, couscous was unknown until some time in the seventh century, when the influence of Arab invaders also saw a wider use of various grains.

Spiced with olives (highly characteristic of North African-Mediterranean cuisine), turmeric, cinnamon, ginger, pine nuts and coriander leaves, lamb tagine, for example, is a poetic, slow-cooked concoction of mutton or lamb braised at a low temperature to ensure tenderness. Tagines are semi-glazed earthenware dishes with pointed, conical lids, used particularly in Moroccan cooking. Although they create aromatic and tasty dishes, don't despair if you don't have one — you can just as easily use an ovenproof casserole dish instead.

In north-east Africa, sweet potatoes are a vitamin-rich, fat-free source of fibre. Baked and sprinkled lightly with sea salt, they make a tasty snack. Ethiopian women still sit cross-legged on the jostling market pavements of Addis Ababa as they have done for centuries, with tiny scales on which they measure out spices with millimetric accuracy for the traditional *wot* (stew cooked in the home). With it, there's sure to be *injera* — a traditional unleavened bread that's still made exactly as it was more than one thousand years ago.

The Turkish invasions of Egypt brought new vitality to Egyptian cooking, and the Egyptians, whose food until then had really been seen as rather bland, were at least able to thank the invaders after the dust had settled for bringing with them a host of tempting delicacies, not least a magnificent dish of garlic prawns with a rhapsodic toasted pine nut couscous.

Hummus — a dip made with crushed chickpeas, tahini, garlic and olive oil, originated from that region over seven thousand years ago. Harissa is a fearsome chilli sauce often used in the preparation of vegetable and meat tagines. Regularly served with couscous, harissa is particularly associated with Tunisia, although it is also enjoyed in Algeria and Morocco.

West African cuisine will be enjoyed by those who like strong sensations, as it is one of volcanic spices, seasonings and bold, assertive flavours. Chillies and tomatoes are staples of the region's culinary repertoire, and the flavours are offset by starchy foods such as cocoyams, yams, root vegetables, cassava, plantains, millet and sorghum.

Staple grains and starches tend to vary from one ethnic group to another. For the purposes of this book, we have adapted a traditional fish recipe to use kingklip in an enticing West African marinade. Served with yam patties and a chickpea salad, it's bound to be a winner at any African-themed dinner party. Also hailing from West Africa, easy-to-prepare chicken *jolof*, a rice-based dish that's often served on special occasions, can't fail to be a sure-fire hit, and has the added advantage that its ingredients make it a complete meal on its own.

Today's West African diet is much heavier in meat (mostly goat), fats and salt than was the case in earlier times, when palm oils and shea butter were used for cooking, and local green vegetables were the dietary staple. Eggs, chicken and guinea fowl are still preferred in the region, and today many dishes combine both fish and meat, usually flaked in the case of fish and heavily spiced.

Unlike North Africa, countries such as Ghana, The Gambia, Nigeria, Togo, Mali, Sierra Leone, Benin, Senegal, Guinea and Côte d'Ivoire — which make up the amorphous region that's generally lumped together as 'West Africa' — didn't absorb nearly as much culinary tradition from their inevitable European settlers as other areas did. In terms of food, this region is better known for its exports rather than the inward influences on its domestic cuisine. Unhappily, when the slave trade was at its height, it was largely these countries whose populations found themselves ignominiously and cruelly shipped all over the world as slaves, principally to the southern states of the United States of America. To this day, anyone who has grown up in the southern US enjoys dishes such as gumbo (a spicy stew), which has its origins in West Africa.

Southern Africa, with its multiple colonial influences and periodic avalanches of indentured labourers and other hopeful immigrants to the area, has a rich and diverse gastronomic heritage. Given such a history, the region could hardly fail to offer an exciting culinary range, but there's no doubt that across all cultures the favourite is meat, and the preferred meat is beef. The Indian and Malay influences, just as they did in parts of East Africa, added spicy curries of varying degrees of ferocity (some of them are not for the faint-hearted; there are explosive blends of curry powder with names like 'razor blade', 'hell-fire' and 'mother-in-law', which will ream the inexperienced from end to end), intriguing *sambals* (chutneys and other traditional accompaniments served with curry), pickled fish and marvellously subtle and flavoursome stews, known locally as *bredies*.

Predictably, perhaps, it is in the Southern African region that the influence of western commercialism is most strongly felt, and the diet of many populations of the south, especially in the cities, is a Western one.

Historically, milk was one of the most important components of the Southern African diet, where cattle were, and in some areas still are, considered a man's most important possession. The old tradition of *lobola* still exists here — an appropriate bride-price, or dowry, that a young man bent on marriage must pay to the father of his would-be bride. Before the advent of refrigeration, however, most milk quickly soured into a kind of yoghurt. Today, many black South Africans enjoy commercial sour milk products, comparable to buttermilk, yoghurt and sour cream.

Invariably served with saffron rice, traditional South African *bobotie* reputedly found its savoury and aromatic way to the southern tip of the continent by courtesy of the Dutch East India Company, which picked up the recipe in Batavia. Known in the Cape since the seventeenth century, the original recipe called for a blend of mutton and pork, whereas today the preferred ingredients are lamb or beef. Quick and easy to make, *bobotie* is a super-subtle, gently spiced culinary symphony of lightly curried mincemeat with a savoury custard topping. Since 1994, Southern African — and South African in particular — cuisine has enjoyed a global resurgence of interest.

To reinforce the simplicity with which everyday foods can be given a uniquely ethnic twist, African pot-roast chicken with vegetables, in the poultry section of this book, would be little more than an everyday Irish stew using chicken instead of lamb or mutton — if it were not for the simple addition of sliced banana.

The versatile plantain is a staple of African cooking. Resembling a banana, the rubbery leaves of the plantain tree are used in rural cookery for steaming meat, fish and poultry. Although they can be eaten either when they are green and bland, or when they are a little overripe and hence sweeter, plantains are firmer and lower in sugar content than ordinary dessert bananas, and therefore ideal for a subtly-spiced beef, plantain and vegetable soup. Deep-fried plantain chips have become popular in recent years.

Peri-peri means 'very hot' in Swahili and Lingana. The widely-loved, nuclear-strength sauce made its eye-watering way into the African culinary repertoire hundreds of years ago when the first European explorers, on their way from the Far East via the Cape of Good Hope, came ashore in Mozambique in search of food and brought with them a fiery chilli of reputed Brazilian parentage. They passed the secrets of its use and the art of blending it with other spices on to the local people. The plant flourished in Africa, and the rest, as they say, is history.

Washed, chopped, steamed or boiled, vitamin-rich and drought-resistant maize, cassava, beans, yams and millet are probably the five most plentiful traditional vegetables on the continent and are usually eaten as an accompaniment to a meat stew. Beans also provide a secondary source of protein.

Tastes of Africa seeks to counter a perception that African cooking is merely a meat-and-two-veg deal, perhaps accompanied by some sort of arbitrary soup and eaten with an uninspiring gravy. Certainly meat, fish and poultry are staples; however in many parts of rural Africa these commodities are relatively easy to obtain and as such have been responsible for the tasty simplicity of its varied traditional dishes.

Spiced with easy-to-make recipes, *Tastes of Africa* is more than just another African cookbook — it's a richly-illustrated hymn to the cuisine, culture and traditions of a continent whose variety, natural hospitality and generosity of spirit are as high, wide and handsome as the sun that travels the hot, timeless and hammered blue-chrome sky that arches overhead.

STARTERS

FISHERMAN'S SOUP

Traditionally throughout Africa, fishermen returning from a fishing expedition sell their catch to locals who, more often than not, request that the fishermen remove the heads. The fishermen are therefore often left with many heads and use their initiative to make a soup.

2 yellowtail heads, washed
4 cups water
1 onion, chopped
1 clove garlic, crushed
1 stick celery, diced
2 potatoes, peeled and cubed
2 cups fresh cream
salt and pepper

Boil the fish heads in the water until soft (± 40 minutes). Strain and reserve the stock, but discard the heads.
Sauté the onion, garlic and celery for 5 minutes, until soft.
Pour in the stock and leave to simmer for 5 minutes. Add the potatoes and simmer until they are cooked (± 10 minutes). Stir in the cream and simmer for a further 5 minutes. Season to taste with salt and pepper. **SERVES 4–6**

CRAYFISH SOUP

If you want to impress dinner guests, this crayfish (or rock lobster) soup is ideal as a first course when serving meat or curry dishes.

1 kg fresh crayfish tails, digestive tract removed
4 cups water
½ onion, chopped
1 carrot, peeled and diced
2 cloves garlic, crushed
30 g butter
4 ripe tomatoes, peeled and diced
½ cup white wine
½ cup fresh cream
salt and pepper

Boil the crayfish in the water for 5 minutes, then remove and leave to cool (but do not discard the water). Peel off the shells, then slice the tails into 4 pieces each.
Fry the onion, carrot and garlic in the butter for 5 minutes. Add the tomatoes and simmer for another 5 minutes. Pour in the white wine and the water from the cooked crayfish. Simmer for 10 minutes, then add the cream and sliced crayfish. Season to taste. **SERVES 4–6**

CHUNKY CHICKEN AND LENTIL SOUP

Chicken dishes are immensely popular in Africa. If cooked properly, chicken stays tender and is therefore easily incorporated into a vegetable soup. Lentils add bulk to this soup while the leeks, celery and mushrooms add their individual flavours, resulting in an interesting and tasty combination.

50 g butter
2 carrots, peeled and chopped
2 onions, chopped
2 leeks, chopped
2 sticks celery, chopped
100 g mushrooms, chopped
6 Tbsp white wine
6 cups chicken stock
½ tsp ground cumin
100 g brown lentils
200 g cooked chicken, diced
salt and pepper

In a large pot, melt the butter and then sauté the carrots, onions, leeks, celery and mushrooms for 5 minutes. Pour in the wine and chicken stock and bring to the boil for 5 minutes. Add the cumin and lentils, cook for 20 minutes, then stir in the chicken. Season to taste and serve hot. **SERVES 4–6**

SWEET POTATO AND COCONUT SOUP

The sweet potato is one of Africa's typical starches, while coconut palms are to be found in many parts of Africa. Very often coconuts form part of meals for special occasions. This combination makes a delicious soup.

1 onion, chopped
1 leek, sliced
1 clove garlic, crushed
¼ tsp ground ginger
3 Tbsp butter
2 sweet potatoes, peeled and diced
2 cups chicken stock
2 cups coconut cream or coconut milk
cayenne pepper

Sauté the onion, leek, garlic and ginger in the butter for 5 minutes. Add the sweet potatoes, chicken stock and coconut cream or coconut milk, and simmer for 10 minutes. Sprinkle with cayenne pepper and serve immediately. **SERVES 4–6**

SWEETCORN AND COCONUT SOUP

Yet another soup enhanced by the inclusion of coconut, the sweetcorn kernels in this creamy mixture plus the flavour of the chilli create a taste sensation!

1 onion, chopped
1 fresh green chilli, chopped
2 Tbsp butter
1–2 yellow mealies (sweetcorn cobs), kernels cut off the cob
¼ tsp dried tarragon
3 cups vegetable stock
¾ cup coconut cream

Sauté the onion and chilli in the butter until soft. Add the rest of the ingredients and simmer for 15 minutes. **SERVES 4–6**

BEEF, PLANTAIN AND VEGETABLE SOUP

Plantains generally need to be cooked or processed in some manner, as opposed to bananas which are eaten raw. They can be used when green or under-ripe and are starchy, or when they are overripe and are sweeter. Because they are firmer and lower in sugar content than dessert bananas, they are ideal for this soup. However, if plantains aren't available, 2 green bananas could be used as a substitute.

500 g beef, cubed
2 Tbsp vegetable oil
2 onions, sliced
2 cloves garlic, crushed
1 tsp ground cumin
1 tsp ground coriander
3 ripe tomatoes, peeled and chopped
5 cups beef stock
2 carrots, peeled and sliced
100 g green beans, sliced into 1-cm lengths
½ plantain or 2 green bananas, peeled and diced
100 g okra
100 g fresh peas, shelled
salt and pepper

Heat the beef with the vegetable oil in a saucepan over high heat and stir-fry until light brown. Add the onions and stir until they are soft, then add the garlic, cumin, coriander and tomatoes and cook for 10 minutes.

Pour in the beef stock, followed by the carrots, green beans and plantain or bananas, and leave to simmer for 5 minutes before adding the okra and peas. Cook for another 5 minutes, then season with the salt and pepper. **SERVES 4–6**

Sweetcorn and coconut soup (back), and
Beef, plantain and vegetable soup (front)

TOMATO AND MEATBALL SOUP

These are meatballs with a difference and combined with the tomato-flavoured soup they offer an unusual African soup. Because tomatoes are grown throughout Africa, they are highly favoured as an ingredient in cooking.

500 g minced beef
2 cloves garlic, crushed
1 Tbsp chopped fresh parsley
1 tsp ground cumin
1 Tbsp vegetable oil
2 large onions, sliced
2 carrots, peeled and sliced
1 Tbsp tomato paste
8 cups beef stock
1 large potato, peeled and chopped
2 large tomatoes, peeled and chopped
4 spring onions, chopped

In a bowl, combine the mince, garlic, parsley and half of the cumin. Shape into small balls, then set aside.
Heat the oil in a large pan and fry the onions until soft. Stir in the remaining cumin, carrots and tomato paste and pour in the stock. Simmer for 20 minutes.
Add the meatballs and potato, then simmer for 10 minutes. Finally, add the tomatoes and spring onions and simmer for a further 5 minutes. **SERVES 4–6**

PERI-PERI CHICKEN LIVERS

Portuguese seafarers were the first people from Europe to set foot in Southern Africa. As they sailed to and from the Far East around the Cape of Good Hope, they would drop anchor in bays along what now forms the Mozambican and South African coastline in order to search for fresh food. It is thought that they introduced a chilli of Brazilian origin to their cooking and in turn passed this on to the local people of Mozambique. The plant thrived in Africa and is one of the most fiery as well as popular of spices in African cuisine.

2 onions, finely chopped
3 Tbsp olive oil
1 tsp cayenne pepper
500 g chicken livers
3 Tbsp brandy
salt and pepper

In a frying pan, sauté the onions in the oil until soft. Add the cayenne pepper and livers and fry over a high heat until cooked. Stir in the brandy, salt and pepper, and stir-fry to combine the flavours. Serve immediately. **SERVES 4–6**

Tomato and meatball soup

YAM PATTIES

Yams are grown in many countries across Africa and feature in a wide variety of African recipes – both sweet and savoury. In Nigeria the yam is known as adamwanga, which means 'Adamo's food'. Folklore has it that Chief Adamo consumed such huge amounts of food, especially yams, that he was banished from his village! If you cannot find yams, potatoes or sweet potatoes will serve as a substitute. If you use sweet potatoes, because they are softer than yams, add another 2 tablespoons of cake flour.

500 g yams, peeled and cubed
1 onion, chopped
2 tsp chopped fresh parsley
2 Tbsp melted butter
1 egg, lightly beaten
2 Tbsp cake flour
salt
flour for dusting
vegetable oil or butter for frying

Boil the yams for 15 minutes, or until soft. Mash, then add the rest of the ingredients, except the flour for dusting and the oil. Use 2 tablespoons of the mixture and roll between the palms of your hands to form a patty, then continue in the same manner with the rest of the mixture. Dust the patties with flour. Heat the oil or butter in a frying pan and fry the patties on both sides until they are golden brown. Serve immediately with a green salad. **SERVES 4–6**

Tiger prawns with peri-peri dip

TIGER PRAWNS WITH PERI-PERI DIP

Because the hot peri-peri flavour is in the dip, delicate palates will also be able to enjoy these unusually flavoured fried prawns.

24 tiger prawns, peeled and deveined, with tails on
2 cups vegetable oil for frying

MARINADE
juice of 3 lemons
¼ cup olive oil
a large pinch each of salt and pepper

COATING
1 cup fresh breadcrumbs
1 cup desiccated coconut
4 eggs, lightly beaten
2 cups cake flour

DIPPING SAUCE
½ cup mayonnaise
½ cup plain yoghurt
1 tsp crushed garlic
1 tsp lemon juice
1 tsp Tabasco
1 tsp chilli powder
1 Tbsp chopped chives or coriander leaves

Combine the marinade ingredients and pour over the prawns. Marinate for 30 minutes.

In a bowl, mix together the breadcrumbs and coconut. Place the beaten eggs in a second bowl and the flour in a third. Dip the prawns in the flour, then in the eggs, and then in the coconut and breadcrumb mixture. Refrigerate for 30 minutes.

Mix together the dipping sauce ingredients and spoon into a serving bowl. Heat the vegetable oil and deep-fry the prawns for 2 minutes. Serve with the dipping sauce. **SERVES 4–6**

SUMMER CHICKEN SALAD

Maize, also known as corn-on-the-cob or mealies, is one of Africa's food staples. This is a simple-to-make and most attractive salad.

2 firm butter lettuces
4 chicken breasts, grilled in a cast-iron griddle pan
1 large yellow mealie on the cob, cooked and kernels removed
2 red onions, cut into wedges
2 firm ripe tomatoes, cut into wedges
1 apple, cut into wedges
2 avocados, thickly sliced lengthways
100 g cheddar cheese, diced

SALAD DRESSING
¼ cup olive oil
⅓ cup lemon juice
3 Tbsp red wine vinegar
2 tsp mustard seeds
1 tsp brown sugar
½ tsp salt

To make the salad dressing, mix all the ingredients in a bowl and whisk lightly. Leave to stand for 10 minutes; this will allow the flavour to develop.
In the meanwhile, separate the lettuce leaves. Wash them, dry thoroughly and arrange on a platter.
Cut each chicken breast into 4 slices and put them in a large bowl with the mealie kernels, onions, tomatoes and apple wedges. Toss gently with half of the salad dressing. Place the chicken mixture on top of the lettuce leaves, then arrange the avocado slices over and around the salad.
Sprinkle with the cheese and drizzle with the remaining salad dressing. **SERVES 4–6**

AVOCADO AND PRAWN SALAD

There are many different types of avocado grown in Africa. For this recipe a fairly small variety would be ideal as it is somewhat of a filling dish.

3 avocados, halved and depipped
salt and pepper
6 large lettuce leaves
400 g shelled and cooked prawns
chopped fresh parsley to garnish

DRESSING
1 cup mayonnaise
3 Tbsp lemon juice
1 Tbsp tomato sauce
¼ tsp cayenne pepper

Season the avocados with the salt and pepper. Place a lettuce leaf on each of 6 plates, followed by an avocado half. Combine the dressing ingredients and then add the prawns. Fill the avocado halves with the prawns and dressing. Garnish with the parsley and serve immediately. **SERVES 6**

Avocado and prawn salad

CHICKEN SKEWERS WITH PEANUT SAUCE

Today's peanut butter is a processed version of the manner in which the indigenous people of Africa utilise groundnuts. The women pound their dried nuts in a huge mortar and then sieve the result to obtain a fine powder that is used as flavouring in their cooking. Peanut butter makes life a lot easier!

8 chicken breasts, cubed
6 bamboo skewers (see page 69)
3 Tbsp vegetable oil
1 onion, finely chopped
2 cloves garlic, chopped
½ cup smooth peanut butter
½ cup chicken stock
¼ tsp cayenne pepper

Preheat the grill. Thread the chicken onto the skewers. In a saucepan, heat the oil and sauté the onion and garlic until soft. Add the peanut butter, chicken stock and cayenne pepper, stirring until the peanut butter has melted. Pour the sauce over the chicken skewers, then place them under the grill, basting regularly with the sauce until cooked. Alternatively, you could cook them in a cast-iron griddle pan or over hot coals on an open fire. **SERVES 4–6**

ROASTED VEGETABLE SALAD

This is currently a very trendy salad and can be made with any seasonal, locally grown vegetables of your choice.

1 cup diced butternut
1 cup sliced (lengthways) carrots
1 cup diced red pepper
1 cup diced green pepper
1 onion, quartered
1 cup green beans, topped and tailed
1 cup thickly sliced baby marrows (courgettes)
1 cup halved patty pans (custard marrows)
2 Tbsp olive oil
salt and pepper
1 lettuce, separated into leaves
2 Tbsp roasted pine nuts

SALAD DRESSING
5 Tbsp olive oil
2 Tbsp balsamic or red wine vinegar
1 tsp Dijon mustard
salt and pepper

Preheat the oven to 180 °C.
Place all the vegetables in a flat, ovenproof dish. Drizzle with the olive oil and sprinkle with the salt and pepper. Roast for 10–15 minutes, ensuring that the vegetables are cooked but still slightly crunchy.
In the meanwhile, whisk together all the dressing ingredients in a bowl.
Serve the vegetables on a bed of lettuce, sprinkle over the pine nuts and drizzle with the salad dressing. **SERVES 4–6**

Chicken skewers with peanut sauce, and Roasted vegetable salad

SWEETCORN FRITTERS

Corn-on-the-cob, or mealies as they are generally known in Southern Africa, are very popular vegetables. Both yellow and white corn varieties are available, but the yellow ones are considered to be sweeter and their kernels are canned as sweetcorn. Sweetcorn fritters are often served at a 'braai' or barbecue. They can also be served as a side dish to a main meal.

1 x 410 g can whole kernel sweetcorn, drained
1 onion, finely chopped
2 eggs, lightly beaten
50 g very fine cornflake crumbs
1 tsp baking powder
salt
cayenne pepper
2 Tbsp butter
5 Tbsp oil

In a bowl, mix the sweetcorn kernels with the onion, eggs, cornflake crumbs, baking powder, salt and cayenne pepper. Melt the butter and oil in a frying pan and drop in a level tablespoon of the sweetcorn mixture. Fry on both sides until brown. Do the same with the rest of the mixture. If not serving immediately, keep warm until ready to use. **SERVES 4–6**

SPICED CHICKEN AND PRAWN KEBABS

King prawns are fairly large and shouldn't be less than 10 cm in length so that they aren't obscured by the chicken pieces.

6 chicken breasts, cubed
18–24 king prawns, peeled but with tails on
5 Tbsp olive oil
juice of 1 lemon
1 fresh green chilli, finely chopped
¼ tsp cayenne pepper
2 Tbsp chopped fresh parsley
¼ tsp salt
6 bamboo (see page 69) or metal skewers
Harissa Hot Chilli Paste (see page 153) to serve
salad leaves to serve

Place the chicken and prawns in a bowl and marinate with the rest of the ingredients for 30 minutes. Thread the chicken pieces and prawns onto 6 skewers, 3–4 prawns per skewer. Grill in a hot cast-iron griddle pan for 5 minutes on each side, basting regularly with the marinade. Serve on a bed of salad leaves with Harissa Hot Chilli Paste. **SERVES 4–6**

Spiced chicken and prawn kebabs, with Sweetcorn fritters

FALAFEL

Falafel originated in Egypt. It is a type of fried ball or patty that is also popular in Middle Eastern countries, where it is served as a fast food. Made from spiced chickpeas and/or fava beans, falafel can be served as a mezze as well.

150 g dried chickpeas
3 Tbsp lemon juice
2 cloves garlic, crushed
2 tsp turmeric
1 tsp cayenne pepper
2 Tbsp cake flour
¼ tsp salt
4 Tbsp chopped fresh coriander
4 Tbsp vegetable oil
2 Tbsp butter

Soak the chickpeas in a bowl of water overnight, drain, then place the chickpeas in a blender. Add the lemon juice, garlic, turmeric, cayenne pepper, flour and salt. Blend the mixture until it is almost smooth, but still has a chunky texture.
Spoon the mixture into a bowl, add the coriander and form into small balls the size of baby onions.
Heat the oil and butter in a pan. Fry the falafel until they are uniformly brown.
Serve on a bed of lettuce. **SERVES 4–6**

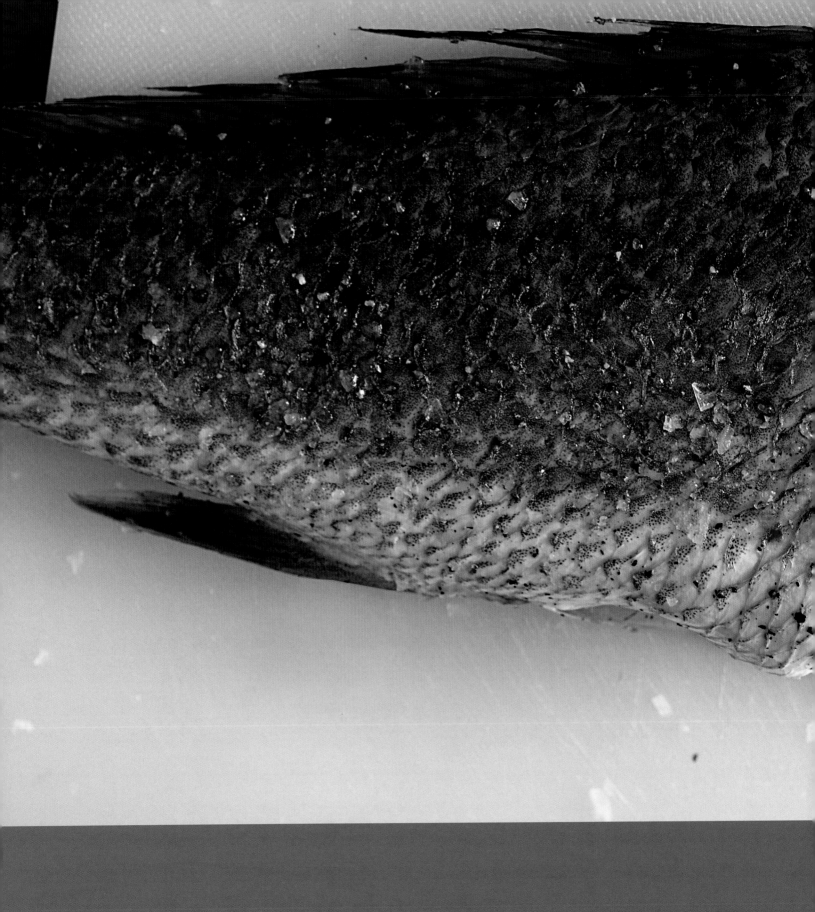

FISH & SEAFOOD

SENEGALESE FISH YASSA

Popular in West Africa, especially in Senegal, 'yassa' refers to spicy, marinated dishes, usually prepared with poultry or fish. Although kingklip is suggested for this recipe, you can substitute it with any firm-fleshed fish. The secret lies in the tangy marinade!

½ cup white wine
½ cup lemon juice
3 Tbsp olive oil
1 Tbsp Dijon mustard
1 fresh green chilli, finely chopped
2 Tbsp chopped fresh parsley
6 kingklip steaks
salt and pepper
flour for dusting
4 Tbsp butter
2 Tbsp cooking oil for frying
4 onions, sliced

Preheat the oven to 200 °C.

Mix together the wine, lemon juice, olive oil, mustard, chilli and parsley in a dish. Marinate the fish steaks in the mixture for 45 minutes. Remove the fish from the marinade and pat dry, but reserve the marinade. Season with the salt and pepper, then dust with the flour.

Heat the butter in a frying pan and brown the fish on both sides – about 3 minutes per side. Transfer the fish steaks to a roasting dish and pour over the reserved marinade.

In the same frying pan add the cooking oil and fry the onions until they caramelise. Spread the onions over the fish in the roasting dish and bake for 10 minutes.

Serve with Yam Patties (see page 21) and a Chickpea Salad with Buttermilk Dressing (see page 141). **SERVES 4–6**

MOROCCAN FRIED CHARMOULA FISH

Charmoula is a traditional Moroccan marinade that is well suited to fish. This is typical street vendor food in North Africa.

6 portions (± 1 kg) yellowtail or kingklip
1 Tbsp coriander seeds
1 tsp turmeric
1 tsp cayenne pepper
1 tsp ground cumin
½ tsp ground ginger
2 fresh green chillies, deseeded and finely chopped
½ cup finely chopped fresh parsley
5 Tbsp butter
4 Tbsp olive oil
1 Tbsp butter
1 cup plain yoghurt
½ cup fresh cream
sea salt

Rinse, then pat dry the fish. Mix together the coriander seeds, turmeric, cayenne pepper, cumin, ginger, chillies and parsley, and coat the fish portions with the mixture.

In a frying pan, heat the 5 tablespoons of butter with the olive oil. Fry the fish until brown on both sides (the time will vary, depending on the thickness of the fish). Remove the fish from the pan and keep it warm.

In the same pan melt the remaining tablespoon of butter, stir in the yoghurt and cream. Heat gently, season to taste with the salt and serve with the warm fish and Charmoula Potatoes (see page 149). **SERVES 4–6**

Senegalese fish yassa, with Yam patties (page 21)

MALAWIAN FISH CURRY

In Malawi this dish is known as sambo yothira kare. *One of the Malawians' favourite fish is chambo. Unfortunately, this particular species is declining in number due to the increase in demand and numbers of fishermen, as fish selling is viewed as an alternative to subsistence agriculture. Normally, chambo is used to make this special dish, but any firm white fish will work well.*

1.5 kg firm white fish, filleted
flour for dusting
vegetable oil for frying
2 onions, chopped
1 green pepper, diced
1 red pepper, diced
1 fresh (preferably green) chilli, chopped
3 Tbsp curry powder
1 clove garlic, crushed
1 tsp ground ginger
1 x 410 g can peeled tomatoes or 4 large fresh tomatoes, peeled
salt and pepper

Gut and clean the fish (or ask your fishmonger to do this when buying the fish). Dry thoroughly. Cut it into 3 pieces (head, middle and tail) and dust the portions with the flour. In a pan, heat the oil and fry the fish until brown. Set aside but retain the pan juices.

Heat sufficient oil to cover the bottom of a pot large enough to accommodate the fish. Fry the onions for about 2 minutes, then add the green and red peppers, chilli, curry powder, garlic, ginger and tomatoes. Cook for 5 minutes, then add the fish. Season with the salt and pepper. Pour in the reserved pan juices. Allow to simmer for 10–15 minutes then serve with mealiepap (see page 141) or rice. **SERVES 4–6**

FISH FRIKKADELS WITH WASABI TARTARE SAUCE

Frikkadel is an Afrikaans word from South Africa for a fish cake or a meatball. Combining them with the Japanese wasabi paste makes for an interesting Afro-Japanese fusion with a distinct bite.

3 potatoes
400 g cooked hake fillets, flaked
6 spring onions, finely chopped
3 Tbsp chopped fresh parsley
1 egg, beaten
salt and pepper
100 g cornflake crumbs
butter for frying

WASABI TARTARE SAUCE
1 cup mayonnaise
1 tsp wasabi paste
1 Tbsp chopped fresh parsley
2 Tbsp chopped gherkins
3 Tbsp lemon juice

To make the sauce, combine all the ingredients. Refrigerate until ready to use.

Boil the potatoes in their jackets until cooked (15–20 minutes). Leave them to cool before peeling, then mash. Combine with the fish, spring onions, parsley, egg, and salt and pepper. Shape into balls (approximately 15) and pat them flat with the palms of your hands. They should have the circumference of a small coffee cup or a medium biscuit cutter. Coat the patties with the cornflake crumbs and fry them in butter until brown.

Serve the frikkadels with the sauce and a salad of your choice.
SERVES 4–6

Fish frikkadels with wasabi tartare sauce

FISH IN BANANA LEAVES WITH ONION AND TOMATO SALSA

While bananas, green or ripe, are an African staple, the fresh leaves are a popular cooking tool as they help to retain moisture and impart delicious flavour. If you can't find a banana leaf, you could use foil, but obviously that won't create the same flavour effect. This dish is traditionally cooked over an open fire.

1 whole kabeljou
1 small banana leaf
salt and pepper
1 onion, thinly sliced
2 lemons, sliced
¼ cup melted butter

SALSA
6 tomatoes, chopped
1 onion, chopped
2 Tbsp chopped fresh parsley
½ fresh chilli, chopped
2 Tbsp olive oil
1 Tbsp vinegar
salt and pepper

To make the salsa, combine all the ingredients in a bowl.
Gut and clean the fish. Prepare the fire.
To soften the banana leaf so that it can fold around the fish, hold the leaf approximately 10 cm above the fire for a few seconds. Once softened, spread it flat on a table. Place the fish on the leaf, ensuring that it will be able to fold over the fish. Season the fish inside and out with the salt and pepper. Arrange the slices of onion and lemon over the top then pour over the butter. Fold the leaf to cover the fish and secure with string.
Place the parcel of fish over the coals for 20 minutes. Check that the flesh is thoroughly cooked, then serve with Roasted Rosemary Potatoes (see page 146). **SERVES 4–6**

CAPE KEDGEREE

Cape Kedgeree has its origins in a dish that the Dutch brought to the Cape from Batavia, along with spices from the East, in the eighteenth century. This is a traditional and very economical South African recipe.

3 Tbsp olive oil
¼ tsp ground cumin
¼ tsp coriander seeds
6 cups cooked and flaked white fish
3 cups cooked white rice
6 hard-boiled eggs, cooled and chopped
salt and pepper
½ cup hot milk
½ lettuce, leaves torn

Heat the oil in a large pan and fry the cumin and coriander for 30 seconds, then add the fish and rice. Gently mix in 5 of the chopped eggs. Season with the salt and pepper, pour in the hot milk and heat through. Arrange the lettuce leaves on a platter and spoon the fish mixture over the lettuce. Grate the remaining chopped egg and garnish the fish with it. **SERVES 4–6**

CITRUS-BAKED HADDOCK

Haddock is lean, easily digestible and lends itself to many cooking methods. Citrus fruits are a key ingredient in Moroccan cooking and this dish is influenced by a Moroccan dish, although in the original a fish stock would be used instead of wine, for religious reasons. In this recipe the white wine, as well as the citrus fruit, does add zing to a simple meal.

1 lemon, sliced
1 lime, sliced
1 orange, sliced
6 haddock fillets
juice of 1 lemon
juice of 1 orange
¾ cup white wine
4 Tbsp chopped fresh parsley
sea salt and freshly ground black pepper
¼ cup sour cream

Preheat the oven to 200 °C. Grease a shallow baking tray. Arrange the sliced fruit in the baking tray. Place the fish fillets over the fruit slices in a single layer. Mix together the lemon juice, orange juice and wine and pour over the fish. Sprinkle the parsley on top, followed by the salt and pepper. Bake for 15 minutes. Transfer the fish to another dish and keep warm.
Pour all the cooking liquid into a saucepan and bring it to the boil. Stir in the sour cream, then pour over the fish. Serve with Sweetcorn Fritters (see page 26). **SERVES 4–6**

KABELJOU WITH HUMMUS AND BROCCOLI

Also called kob, kabeljou is known as 'the meagre' in the United Kingdom and the 'omber-visch' in The Netherlands. It is an excellent eating fish, but its numbers are also, unfortunately, under pressure from over-fishing.

6 kabeljou fillets
salt
1 fresh green chilli, finely chopped
flour for dusting
4 Tbsp vegetable oil
1 cup hummus (see page 154)
1 kg broccoli florets, cooked but firm

Season the fish with the salt and green chilli, then dust with the flour. Heat the oil in a frying pan and fry the fish on both sides (about 5 minutes per side) until cooked. Spread a thick layer of hummus over the flesh side, then cover with the broccoli. Serve with roasted sweet potatoes. **SERVES 4–6**

RED ROMAN WITH OLIVE SAUCE

This reef fish is found along the southern and eastern coasts of Africa and is a popular catch with anglers. In this recipe, red roman can be substituted with yellowtail or snoek.

2 red romans, filleted
sea salt
3 onions, sliced into rings
olive oil for drizzling

SAUCE
100 g black olives
2 cups vegetable stock
¼ cup olive oil
¼ cup chopped fresh parsley
3 Tbsp red wine vinegar
1 Tbsp prepared mild mustard
salt and pepper

Preheat the grill.
Season the fish with the sea salt. Arrange the onion rings in an ovenproof baking dish and place the fish on top. Drizzle with the olive oil. Grill for 10 minutes until cooked, then keep warm. Combine all the sauce ingredients in a blender until smooth. Heat the sauce in a saucepan then pour into a serving dish and place the fish on top.
Serve with boiled baby potatoes. **SERVES 4–6**

KINGKLIP WITH MUSHROOMS AND GREEN OLIVES

Kingklip is one of the most delicious fish from Southern Africa. Trawled in deep waters, it has suffered from overfishing and is also expensive, so should preferably be reserved for special occasions. Suitable for sautéing, oven baking, poaching, grilling or frying, the firm-textured flesh flakes into chunks when cooked.

3 Tbsp vegetable oil
1 onion, chopped
1 red pepper, chopped
5 ripe tomatoes, peeled and puréed
200 g mushrooms, quartered
½ cup white wine
1½ cups fish stock or vegetable stock
100 g green olives, sliced
salt and pepper
6 kingklip steaks or any firm, white fish
sea salt
4 Tbsp butter

Heat the oil in a saucepan and sauté the onion and red pepper for 5 minutes. Pour in the puréed tomatoes and simmer for a further 5 minutes. Add the mushrooms, wine and fish stock or vegetable stock and cook, uncovered, for 10 minutes over a low heat. Add the olives and season to taste. Remove the saucepan from the heat.

Dry the fish thoroughly and season with the salt. In a frying pan, heat the butter and fry the fish on both sides until brown. Spoon the sauce into a serving dish (with some depth) and place the fish on top.

Serve with mashed potatoes and Green Bean and Tomato Salad (see page 134). **SERVES 4–6**

Kingklip with mushrooms and green olives

PAN-FRIED SALMON WITH SWEETCORN SALSA

The sweetcorn salsa adds a uniquely African twist to the salmon.

5 salmon steaks
salt
3 Tbsp sesame seeds
4 Tbsp butter

SALSA
2 cups cooked sweetcorn
300 g tomatoes, chopped
5 spring onions, chopped
1 fresh green chilli, chopped
2 Tbsp chopped coriander leaves
3 Tbsp olive oil
3 Tbsp vinegar or lemon juice
½ tsp salt

Mix all the salsa ingredients, then set aside to allow the flavour to develop.

Season the salmon with the salt and sprinkle the sesame seeds over the fleshy side. Heat the butter and fry the salmon on both sides – approximately 4 minutes per side, depending on the thickness of the fillets. Serve with the sweetcorn salsa and a green salad. **SERVES 4–6**

TUNA VINDAYE WITH BABY ONIONS

Traditionally flavoured with mustard, bay leaves, garlic and chillies, vindaye is a dish from the island of Mauritius, off the coast of East Africa.

2 bay leaves, crumbled
1 fresh green chilli, chopped
3 Tbsp yellow mustard seeds, crushed
4 Tbsp black peppercorns, crushed
5 cloves garlic, crushed
4 Tbsp chopped fresh parsley
6 tuna steaks
salt
5 Tbsp butter
3 Tbsp olive oil
12 baby onions, peeled
⅓ cup red or white wine vinegar

Mix together the bay leaves, chilli, mustard seeds, peppercorns, garlic and parsley. Season the tuna steaks with salt, and coat with half of the spice mixture.

In a frying pan, heat 3 tablespoons of the butter and oil and fry the tuna for 3–4 minutes on each side, then remove, but keep warm. In the same pan add the remaining butter and fry the onions until they are light brown and cooked through. Stir in the remaining spice mixture, pour in the vinegar and return the tuna steaks to the pan. Turn the tuna and heat through. Serve with Brinjal Salad (see page 140). **SERVES 4–6**

Tuna vindaye with baby onions, and Brinjal salad (page 140)

TUNA WITH MASHED PEAS AND FRESH HERB SAUCE

Tuna (or tunny) is a large, firm-fleshed game fish found along the South African Cape coast from Saldanha to Cape Hangklip.

6 tuna steaks
4 Tbsp chopped fresh parsley
grated rind of 2 lemons
sea salt
2 Tbsp crushed black peppercorns
4 Tbsp butter

TOPPING
400 g shelled peas, cooked
2 Tbsp melted butter
salt and pepper

SAUCE
½ cup parsley leaves
½ cup coriander leaves
4 spring onions, chopped
2 cloves garlic
3 Tbsp capers
¼ cup olive oil
4 Tbsp lemon juice

Pat the tuna dry. Combine the parsley, lemon rind, sea salt and crushed peppercorns, then coat the fish with the mixture. Heat the 4 tablespoons of butter in a frying pan and brown the fish on both sides, about 5 minutes per side. For the topping, purée the peas and butter in a blender until just blended and season to taste. Spoon the topping over the tuna and grill for 5 minutes. In the meanwhile, blend all the sauce ingredients until smooth. Place the fish in a serving dish and pour the sauce around the fish. Serve with Sweet Potato Chips (see page 150). **SERVES 4–6**

BRAAIED SNOEK FILLETS WITH MUSTARD-DILL SAUCE

Snoek is a silvery-coloured, oily fish. Braaied (or barbecued) snoek is traditional to the Cape in South African cuisine. Fresh is always best, if it's in season, otherwise look for frozen snoek.

3 snoek fillets
½ cup olive oil
1 Tbsp sea salt
grated rind of 1 lemon

SAUCE
¼ cup chicken stock
1 cup fresh cream
½ cup cream cheese
2 tsp Dijon mustard
2 tsp hot English mustard powder
2 Tbsp water
1 Tbsp chopped fresh dill
2 tsp lime juice or 2 Tbsp lemon juice
salt and pepper

Prepare an open fire with coals suitable for braaing the fish. Cut the fillets in half and place them in a bowl. Combine the oil, salt and lemon rind, then pour over the fish and marinate for 1 hour.

In a saucepan, heat the chicken stock, then add the fresh cream and cream cheese. Stir until the cream cheese is completely dissolved.

Mix together the Dijon mustard and English mustard powder with the water and stir until smooth. Pour into the cream sauce, add the dill and lime juice and season with salt and pepper.

Place the fish in a closing braai grid and braai over the coals until brown, basting regularly with the sauce.

Serve with Sweet Potato Chips (see page 150). **SERVES 4–6**

MOZAMBICAN SPICED CALAMARI

Portuguese trading settlements first appeared on the coast of the area that is now Mozambique some 500 years ago. The Portuguese gradually moved further inland and by the 1890s this land fell under Portuguese colonial administration. Mozambique gained its independence in 1975, but after such a lengthy period it's unsurprising that the country's cooking has been greatly influenced by Portuguese cuisine.

3 Tbsp butter
700 g calamari rings
4 Tbsp crushed garlic
1 tsp fresh ginger, finely chopped
1 tsp fresh green chilli, finely chopped
grated rind of 1 lemon

SAUCE
1 onion, chopped
1 cup lemon juice
1 cup white wine
3 Tbsp soy sauce
1 Tbsp brown sugar

Heat the butter in a frying pan. Fry the calamari for 2 minutes and then add the garlic, ginger, chilli and lemon rind. Fry for a further 2 minutes.

Mix together the sauce ingredients and pour into the pan with the calamari. Allow to boil for 3 minutes. Remove the calamari and cook until the sauce has reduced by half. In the meanwhile, keep the calamari warm. Once the sauce is ready, combine it with the calamari.

Serve with rice or potato chips. **SERVES 4–6**

Mozambican spiced calamari

OYSTERS MOMBASA WITH LEMON-DILL SAUCE

There aren't many African recipes featuring oysters and it is thought that this particular recipe was introduced by the British expatriates into Kenya during the days of colonialism. Their gateway to the 'white highlands' and Happy Valley of Kenya was Mombasa on the east coast of Africa. The new settlers initiated various exotic dishes and to this day Kenyan oysters are the ones to buy if possible.

24 medium fresh oysters, opened

SAUCE
100 g butter
50 g cake flour
1 cup fish stock or light chicken stock
¼ cup lemon juice
¾ cup fresh cream
2 Tbsp dried dill
salt and pepper
lemon wedges to garnish

In a saucepan, melt half the butter and gradually stir in the flour. Keep stirring until the flour starts to turn a caramel colour. Add the stock little by little in three stages, stirring continuously. Add the lemon juice, still stirring, then add the cream and dill. Whisk in the remaining butter. Season with salt and pepper. Arrange the oysters on a bed of crushed ice, garnish with the lemon wedges and serve with the sauce. The sauce may be served hot or cold. **SERVES 4–6**

CAPE CALAMARI STUFFED WITH FETA AND SPINACH

Calamari is the Italian name for squid. The feta cheese, spinach and pine nuts in this recipe complement the firm, white flesh of the calamari with its slightly sweet, almost nutty flavour.

300 g feta cheese
500 g baby spinach
4 spring onions, finely chopped
4 Tbsp toasted pine nuts
2 Tbsp melted butter
salt and pepper
4–6 calamari tubes

Crumble the feta into a bowl. Wash the spinach and place it in a pot of boiling water until it just starts to wilt. Allow it to cool then squeeze out all the water. Mix the spinach with the feta. Add the onions, pine nuts and melted butter, then season with the salt and pepper. Blend the mixture until it is smooth, then stuff the calamari tubes with it.
Heat a cast-iron pan until hot. Brush the calamari with oil and grill until brown all over. Serve with potato chips. **SERVES 4–6**

Oysters Mombasa with lemon-dill sauce

EAST AFRICAN PRAWN STIR-FRY

Prawns are fished in the Indian Ocean from Southern Africa right up to East Africa. Foreign prawn trawlers are banned by some of the East African countries as the industry is protected for their artisanal fishermen.

4 Tbsp olive oil
1 onion, chopped
2 cloves garlic, crushed
1 red pepper, cut into strips
1 green pepper, cut into strips
2 carrots, peeled and julienned
100 g okra, tops removed and washed
200 g button mushrooms, sliced
300 g prawns, shelled and deveined
3 slices fresh ginger, finely chopped
1 fresh green chilli, finely chopped
¼ cup soy sauce
¼ cup lemon juice
¼ cup sweet chilli sauce
salt and pepper

In a large frying pan, heat the oil and fry the onion for 3 minutes. Add the garlic, all the vegetables, prawns, ginger and green chilli and stir-fry for 3 minutes over high heat. Add the remaining ingredients and stir-fry for a further 3 minutes. Serve with rice or couscous. **SERVES 4–6**

PRAWNS WITH AVOCADO AND CASHEW NUT SALAD

Mozambique provides the backdrop to this delicious salad. A handy tip is to blanch unpeeled avocados in boiling water for a few seconds to prevent them from turning black.

3 Tbsp olive oil
250 g prawns, shelled and deveined but with tails on
1 fresh green chilli, finely chopped
4 cloves garlic, crushed
6 spring onions, sliced
100 g fresh peas, shelled
1 Tbsp chopped fresh parsley
2 avocados, peeled and cubed
100 g cashew nuts, toasted
1 Tbsp mayonnaise
salt and pepper
crisp lettuce to serve

In a frying pan, heat the oil and fry the prawns for 2 minutes. Add the chilli, garlic, spring onions and peas and stir-fry for 3 minutes. Remove the pan from the heat. Once cool, add the parsley, avocados, cashew nuts and mayonnaise. Season with the salt and pepper and serve on a bed of lettuce, along with a crusty bread. **SERVES 4–6**

Prawns with avocado and cashew nut salad

MUSSELS IN WHITE WINE GARLIC SAUCE

This fabulous seafood dish is very impressive although it's so simple to produce. It's a tradition along the Cape West Coast for people to collect their own mussels and then to prepare this dish. It's much easier to use mussels that have already been cleaned and opened into half shells. If you live at the coast and are collecting your own fresh mussels, boil them in a pot of salted water. When they open, they are ready. Do not use any mussels that have not opened on their own after boiling.

3 Tbsp butter
1 onion, finely chopped
11 cloves garlic, crushed
3 Tbsp cake flour
2 cups white wine
¾ cup fresh cream
30 fresh mussels
½ tsp garlic salt and pepper
1 Tbsp chopped fresh parsley

Heat the butter in a large pot and sauté the onion for 5 minutes. Add the garlic and stir-fry for 1 minute. Stir in the flour, quickly and thoroughly. Pour in the wine and keep stirring to prevent any lumps from forming. (A balloon whisk is useful for breaking up lumps.) Add the cream and mussels and cook slowly for about 10 minutes. Season with the garlic salt and pepper. Just before serving, stir in the parsley. Serve immediately with Savoury Rice (see page 133). **SERVES 4–6**

GARLIC AND CHILLI KING PRAWNS

The best prawns in Southern Africa come from Mozambique and the Portuguese influence of combining chilli and garlic makes them truly irresistible.

24 king prawns
7 cloves garlic, crushed
4 fresh green chillies, finely chopped
4 Tbsp olive oil
4 Tbsp chopped fresh parsley
juice of 1 lemon
salt and pepper

Preheat the grill. Slice the prawns halfway through, lengthways, then butterfly them and press down so that they are flat. Remove the veins. Place the prawns in a roasting pan, flat cut-side up. Mix together the remaining ingredients and then pour over the prawns and leave to stand for 20 minutes. Place under the grill for 5–8 minutes.
Serve with potato chips or rice. **SERVES 4–6**

Mussels in white wine garlic sauce

POULTRY

FRIED CHICKEN BREAST WITH MUSHROOM-SHERRY SAUCE

Do remember that unless you have to remove the skin for health reasons, chicken breasts with the skin intact are more flavoursome. The delicious mushroom and sherry sauce will combat any hint of dryness in the breast meat.

6 chicken breasts with skin on
sea salt and pepper
1 Tbsp butter
2 Tbsp olive oil

SAUCE
2 Tbsp butter
2 Tbsp olive oil
300 g white mushrooms, sliced
3 cloves garlic, crushed
350 ml fresh cream
150 ml medium sherry
salt and pepper

Cut 4 slits into the skin of each chicken breast and season with the sea salt and pepper. In a large frying pan, heat the butter and oil and brown the chicken breasts for 5 minutes on each side. Keep warm.

For the sauce, melt the butter and oil in a saucepan, add the mushrooms and garlic, and stir for 3 minutes. Add the cream, sherry, and salt and pepper, then simmer for 10 minutes. Transfer the chicken pieces to a serving dish and pour the sauce over. Serve with North African Couscous Salad (see page 134) and Roasted Vegetable Salad (see page 25). **SERVES 4–6**

CHICKEN JOLOF

This colourful dish hails from West Africa and is often served on special occasions. Best of all, it is a complete meal in one pot.

2 kg chicken pieces
salt and pepper
3 Tbsp vegetable oil
3 leeks, sliced
2 cloves garlic, crushed
1 fresh green chilli, finely chopped
400 g tomatoes, peeled and chopped
½ cup white wine
2½ cups chicken stock
1 cup uncooked basmati rice
1 cup cubed butternut
200 g fresh shrimps, peeled and deveined
grated rind of 1 lemon
1 Tbsp chopped fresh parsley

Season the chicken with salt and pepper.

Heat the oil in a frying pan and brown the chicken. Transfer the fried chicken pieces to a large pot and set aside. Pour off the excess oil, leaving about 3 tablespoons in the pan. In the same frying pan, sauté the leeks and garlic until just soft, then add the chilli, tomatoes and wine. Simmer for 10 minutes, then stir in the chicken stock and pour all into the pot with the browned chicken. Simmer for a further 10 minutes. Add the rice, stirring gently, then lower the heat, cover and leave to cook for 5 minutes. Add the butternut and after 5–7 minutes, stir in the shrimps. Season with salt and pepper. Just before serving stir in the lemon rind and parsley. **SERVES 4–6**

Chicken jolof

NORTH AFRICAN CHICKEN TAGINE

Tagines are semi-glazed earthenware dishes with pointed, conical lids, particularly used in Moroccan cooking. If you don't have one, use an ovenproof casserole dish instead. Olives are highly characteristic of North African-Mediterranean cuisine.

4 Tbsp vegetable oil
8 chicken drumsticks
2 onions, finely chopped
3 cloves garlic, crushed
1 tsp ground ginger
1 tsp turmeric
1 stick cinnamon
2 cups chicken stock
1 cup pitted green olives
salt and pepper

In a frying pan, heat the oil and brown the chicken pieces, then transfer them to a large pot.
Pour off some of the oil from the frying pan, leaving about 2 tablespoons. Fry the onions in the oil until soft, then add the garlic, ginger, turmeric and cinnamon, and stir-fry for 2 minutes. Pour in the chicken stock and bring to the boil.
Add the onion mixture to the pot of chicken, followed by the olives. Season with the salt and pepper and simmer for 40 minutes.
Serve with couscous and Chickpea and Lentil Salad (see page 140). **SERVES 4–6**

CHICKEN IN GROUND CASHEW NUT SAUCE

Although native to South America, the cashew nut tree was introduced to Africa by Portuguese traders and now these trees grow prolifically in Nigeria, Mozambique, Tanzania and Kenya. The nuts add both nutrition and flavour to this dish.

4 Tbsp olive oil
3 onions, chopped
1 x 410 g can peeled tomatoes
1 Tbsp tomato paste
¼ tsp chilli powder
½ tsp turmeric
1 clove garlic
2 Tbsp chopped fresh coriander
1 cup chicken stock
70 g cashew nuts
6 chicken breasts, cubed
salt and pepper
1 Tbsp plain yoghurt

Heat the oil in a pot and sauté the onions for 3 minutes. Add the tomatoes, tomato paste, chilli powder, turmeric, garlic, coriander and chicken stock, then blend in a food processor until smooth. Return to the pot.
Pound the nuts in a mortar until they are a fine powder and then add to the sauce. Simmer gently for 10 minutes. Add the chicken breasts and simmer for another 10 minutes. Season with the salt and pepper. Just before serving stir in the yoghurt.
Serve with rice. **SERVES 4–6**

North African chicken tagine, with Chickpea and lentil salad (page 140)

CHICKEN WITH PORT AND RAISINS

In Namibia a tradition has developed in which this dish is served for romantic dinners. The port and raisins impart an intriguing sweetish flavour to the chicken.

¼ cup vegetable oil
12 chicken drumsticks
80 g streaky bacon, diced
2 onions, sliced into rings
3 cloves garlic, crushed
1 tsp dried thyme
1 cup port
3 cups chicken stock
½ cup raisins
salt and pepper
10 baby potatoes

Heat the oil in a deep frying pan and brown the chicken for about 10 minutes. Remove from the frying pan and set aside. In the same pan, add the bacon and brown lightly. Add the onions and garlic and sauté until the onions are soft. Stir in the thyme and pour in the port, then boil for 2 minutes. Add the chicken stock and raisins. Place the chicken back into the frying pan and season with the salt and pepper. Simmer, covered, for 20 minutes.

In the meanwhile, boil the baby potatoes in salted water for approximately 7 minutes, or until soft.

Serve the chicken with the boiled potatoes. **SERVES 4–6**

Chicken with port and raisins

MOROCCAN LEMON CHICKEN WITH OLIVES

This traditional dish makes for a quick and easy meal.

4 Tbsp olive oil
2 Tbsp butter
2 kg chicken, cut into pieces (or 12 chicken thighs)
3 onions, finely chopped
2 cloves garlic, crushed
400 g tomatoes, chopped
¼ tsp dried thyme
1 tsp dried rosemary
1 bay leaf
20 pitted green olives
¼ cup lemon juice
salt and pepper
2 cups fresh cream

In a frying pan, heat the oil and butter and brown the chicken pieces, then transfer them to a large pot.

In the same frying pan, reduce the heat and sauté the onions and garlic until soft. Add the tomatoes and sauté them for approximately 7 minutes until soft. Stir in the thyme, rosemary and bay leaf and bring all to the boil.

Add the tomato and herb mixture to the chicken pot, along with the olives, and simmer, covered, for 25 minutes. Stir in the lemon juice and season with the salt and pepper. Just before serving, stir in the cream.

Serve with Savoury Rice (see page 133). **SERVES 4–6**

EAST AFRICAN POT ROAST CHICKEN WITH COCONUT CREAM

It's the combination of coconut cream and chilli that adds oomph to this dish.

2 Tbsp vegetable oil
2 Tbsp butter
1 whole chicken, washed and dried
½ onion, roughly chopped
3 cloves garlic, crushed
1 fresh green chilli, chopped
1 cup chicken stock
1 x 400 g can coconut cream
salt and pepper

Heat the oil and butter in a frying pan and brown the chicken all over. Transfer to a large pot.
In the same frying pan, sauté the onion, garlic and chilli for 5 minutes. Pour in the chicken stock and coconut cream, and bring to the boil. Season with the salt and pepper. Pour the sauce into the pot with the chicken and simmer, covered, for 1 hour.
Serve with Coconut Rice (see page 136). **SERVES 4–6**

MALAWIAN SPICED CHICKEN CURRY

In Malawi this dish is known as nkhuku ya sabola, *which means 'a spicy one'. It is simple to prepare and a favourite for special occasions.*

500 g chicken pieces, with skin on
salt
3–5 Tbsp vegetable oil
3 large onions, chopped
5 tomatoes, peeled and chopped
2 Tbsp curry powder
1 fresh green chilli, chopped
1 tsp dried thyme
1 cup water
2 cups chicken stock
1 cup peeled and cubed potatoes
pepper

Season the chicken pieces with the salt. Heat the oil in a frying pan and fry the pieces until brown, then transfer to a large pot. Pour off most of the oil in the pan, leaving about 2 tablespoons. Sauté the onions until soft. Add the tomatoes, curry powder, chilli and thyme. After a few minutes, pour in the water and stock and bring to the boil. Add the onion mixture to the pot with the chicken. Simmer, covered, for 45 minutes over a very low heat. Add the potatoes and cook for a further 15 minutes. Season to taste with salt and pepper.
Serve with mealiepap (see page 141) or rice, and Malawi's Favourite Cabbage Salad (see page 135). **SERVES 4–6**

Malawian spiced chicken curry

CHICKEN, MUSHROOM AND LEEK PIE

This pie is ideal as a light lunch.

1 x 400 g packet puff pastry
2 Tbsp vegetable oil
1 onion, finely chopped
4 leeks, sliced
1 cup quartered button mushrooms
6 chicken breasts, cooked and cubed
salt and pepper

SAUCE
50 g butter
50 g cake flour
¼ cup white wine
½ cup chicken stock
½ cup fresh cream
1 tsp Dijon mustard
salt and pepper

Preheat the oven to 200 °C and spray a pie dish with cooking spray. Roll the pastry out, cut it in half and line the dish with one one half, ensuring that it reaches to the top of the dish. Heat the oil and sauté the onion and leeks until soft. Add the mushrooms and stir-fry for 3 minutes, then add the chicken. Season with the salt and pepper and set aside.
To make the sauce, heat the butter in a saucepan, then add the flour. Keep stirring until it starts to brown. Pour in the wine and chicken stock and stir until smooth. Add the cream and mustard and keep stirring until well mixed. Season with salt and pepper and cook for 2 minutes. Combine the sauce and chicken mixture, leave to cool then spoon into the pastry case. Cover with the remaining sheet of pastry and pinch the pastry edges together firmly between your fingers. Cut a small vent into the top of the pie to allow steam to escape. Bake for 30 minutes. Serve with a salad of your choice. **SERVES 4–6**

SHEBEEN CHICKEN

Originally a shebeen was an illicit bar in Ireland where unlicenced alcohol was sold. The popularity of shebeens spread to other countries, including South Africa, where many shebeens are now legal. The atmosphere is congenial and lively and this definitely influences the food that is served, washed down with local beer.

6 chicken breasts, skinned and deboned
1–2 tsp chicken spice
6 spinach leaves
1 cup chopped dried apricots, soaked in boiling water for 1 hour
1 onion, chopped and lightly sautéed
1 litre chicken stock

SAUCE
2 Tbsp butter
1 tsp cumin seeds
1 Tbsp minced fresh ginger
1 cup chicken stock
1 stick cinnamon
1 bay leaf
2 Tbsp lemon juice
2 Tbsp coriander leaves

Flatten the chicken breasts with a rolling pin and rub in the spice. Top each breast with a spinach leaf and spread with apricots and sautéed onion. Roll each into a sausage shape and wrap each in clingwrap, sealing at both ends with a knot. Bring the 1 litre chicken stock to the boil and poach the breasts for 15 minutes. Make the sauce in the meanwhile by melting the butter in a pan, stir in the cumin seeds and ginger and cook for 1 minute. Add the cup of chicken stock, cinnamon, bay leaf and lemon juice and simmer for 10 minutes. Remove the cinnamon stick and stir in the coriander leaves. Remove the chicken from the clingwrap and arrange in a serving dish. Pour the sauce over and serve with North African Couscous Salad (see page 134). **SERVES 4–6**

AFRICAN POT ROAST CHICKEN WITH VEGETABLES

This could almost be an Irish stew, but it is given an African touch with the addition of unripe bananas!

2 Tbsp vegetable oil
1 whole chicken
2 cups chicken stock
1 tsp dried thyme
1 tsp turmeric
2 lemon leaves
1 x 410 g can peeled tomatoes
4 carrots, peeled and sliced
2 unripe bananas, peeled and sliced
2 cups shredded cabbage
1 potato, peeled and diced
salt and pepper

In a large pot, heat the oil and brown the chicken. Pour in the chicken stock, then add the thyme, turmeric, lemon leaves and tomatoes. Cover and simmer for 30 minutes, then add the rest of the vegetables. Simmer for a further 10 minutes. Season with the salt and pepper.
Serve with rice. **SERVES 4–6**

TURKEY DRUMSTICKS WITH SHERRY-LIVER SAUCE

Turkeys are reared in many parts of Africa, but not always for the pot as they are regarded as domestic pets in some countries. Only when people have run out of food will they resort to turkey meat, or for the most special of occasions.

3 turkey drumsticks
salt and pepper
12 rashers streaky bacon
olive oil

SAUCE
50 g butter
1 onion, chopped
3 cloves garlic
2 cups chicken stock
2 Tbsp vegetable oil
250 g chicken livers
1 tsp dried thyme
150 ml medium sherry
100 ml cream

Preheat the oven to 180 °C. Season the turkey with the salt and pepper, then wrap about 4 bacon rashers around each drumstick. Place the drumsticks in a roasting dish and drizzle with the olive oil. Roast for approximately 1 hour.
For the sauce, melt the butter in a saucepan, then sauté the onion and garlic until soft. Pour in the chicken stock and simmer for 10 minutes.
In a frying pan, heat the oil until hot and fry the chicken livers until just light brown. Add the thyme and the sherry and cook for 5 minutes. Pour in the onion, garlic and stock mixture and boil for 3 minutes. Stir in the cream, leave to cool and then blend until smooth. Reheat the sauce and serve with the turkey drumsticks and Chickpea and Lentil Salad (see page 140). **SERVES 4–6**

CHICKEN THIGHS AND SPINACH IN PEANUT SAUCE

In Zimbabwe this dish is called dovi*, which is the word for peanut sauce in that country. It is served with mealiepap, also called sadza. If you don't already know, baby marrows are also known as courgettes or zucchini.*

6 chicken thighs
4 Tbsp vegetable oil
3 onions, finely chopped
4 tomatoes, peeled and chopped
½ cup chicken stock
3 baby marrows, sliced ±1 cm thick
¼ cup peanut butter
½ tsp cayenne pepper
500 g shredded fresh spinach
salt

Cut an 'X' into the skin of each chicken thigh. Heat the oil in a frying pan and fry the chicken until well browned. Transfer the thighs to a pot and pour off most of the oil from the frying pan, leaving about 3 tablespoons.

In the same pan, sauté the onions over a low heat until soft, then add the tomatoes and stir until soft. Stir in the chicken stock, then pour this stock mixture into the pot with the chicken and simmer for 15 minutes. Add the baby marrows and peanut butter and stir until the peanut butter has dissolved. Add the cayenne pepper and spinach, and simmer for approximately 5 minutes until the spinach has wilted. Add salt to taste.

Serve with mealiepap. **SERVES 4–6**

CHICKEN AND PRAWN CURRY

This is a popular East African dish known as Kuku Nanazi. Kuku *means 'chicken' and* nanazi *means 'pineapple' in Swahili and Chichewa – one of the languages of Malawi.*

4 Tbsp olive oil
2 onions, finely chopped
4 cloves garlic
1 tsp ground ginger
2 Tbsp curry powder (medium or hot)
6 cardamom seeds
1 tsp turmeric
1–2 fresh green chillies, finely chopped
1 x 400 ml can coconut cream
5–6 skinless chicken breasts, cubed
12 large prawns, shelled and deveined
1 small pineapple, peeled and cubed
salt and pepper

In a large pot, heat the oil and sauté the onions and garlic until soft. Add the ginger, curry powder, cardamom seeds, turmeric and chillies and fry for 3 minutes. Pour in the coconut cream and add the chicken. Simmer gently until the chicken is almost cooked (10–15 minutes), then add the prawns and continue simmering until they are done. Season with the salt and pepper.

Serve with rice. **SERVES 4–6**

Chicken thighs and spinach in peanut sauce

CHICKEN BREYANI

Breyani found its way to Africa via the Indian and Pakistani settlers to the continent. Due to its lengthy preparation, this dish is often served during Ramadan or on special occasions.

1.5 kg skinless chicken pieces
1 cup brown lentils
2 cups uncooked white rice (preferably basmati)
1 tsp turmeric
2 sticks cinnamon
4 cardamom pods
1 cup hot water
2 onions, sliced
4 potatoes, peeled and quartered
1 cup chicken stock

MARINADE

1 cup buttermilk
2 Tbsp vegetable oil
2 Tbsp masala
1 Tbsp turmeric
1 tsp ground cinnamon
1 Tbsp each ground coriander and ground cumin
3 fresh green chillies, chopped
1 Tbsp grated fresh ginger
1½ tsp salt
400 g fresh tomatoes, peeled

Mix all the marinade ingredients together and pour over the chicken pieces until completely covered. Marinate for 2 hours. Boil the lentils in water until tender, then drain. Boil the rice in water with the turmeric, cinnamon and cardamom until cooked. Transfer the chicken and marinade to a large pot. Bring to the boil and simmer, covered, for 20 minutes. Uncover and simmer for another 10 minutes. Add the rice, lentils, onions, potatoes and stock. Simmer for 20 minutes and serve. **SERVES 6–8**

OSTRICH SKEWERS BASTED WITH J'S SPICED FRUIT CHUTNEY

Ostrich meat has a lower fat content than other red meat and is, therefore, healthier and a good choice for those with high cholesterol. Remember to soak bamboo skewers in water for 30 minutes to stop them from burning at either end, or cover them with cooking foil.

600 g ostrich steaks
½ cup J's Spiced Fruit Chutney (see page 154)
1 fresh green chilli, finely chopped
1 Tbsp beef stock powder
2 Tbsp red wine vinegar or 2 Tbsp lemon juice
salt and pepper
1 cup soft-eating dried apricots
6 bamboo skewers

Prepare an open fire with coals suitable for braaing (barbecuing). Cut the steaks into large cubes. Combine J's Spiced Fruit Chutney, the chilli, beef stock powder, vinegar or lemon juice, and salt and pepper. Pour this mixture over the ostrich cubes and marinate for a minimum of 30 minutes. Thread the meat and apricots alternately onto the skewers and braai over hot coals, 5 minutes on each side, basting regularly with the marinade. Serve with Vegetable Fritters with Avocado and Tomato Salsa (see page 121). **SERVES 4–6**

OSTRICH STEAKS WITH SHIITAKE MUSHROOM-TARRAGON SAUCE

The combination of ostrich meat and shiitake mushrooms creates another exotic Afro-Japanese fusion dish.

5–6 ostrich steaks
2 Tbsp butter
6 spring onions, sliced
4 cloves garlic, crushed
juice of 1 lemon
150 g fresh shiitake mushrooms, sliced
1 cup fresh cream
3 Tbsp chopped fresh tarragon
salt and pepper
4 Tbsp butter

Pat dry the ostrich steaks.
In a saucepan, melt the 2 tablespoons of butter and sauté the spring onions and garlic for 5 minutes, or until soft. Add the lemon juice and mushrooms and cook for 3 minutes. Pour in the cream and simmer very gently for 7 minutes, then add the tarragon and season to taste. Keep the sauce warm.
Season the steaks with pepper and pan-fry in the 4 tablespoons of butter, 4–5 minutes on each side.
Serve with the mushroom-tarragon sauce and boiled potatoes.
SERVES 4–6

Ostrich skewers basted with J's spiced fruit chutney, and Vegetable fritters with avocado and tomato salsa (page 121)

OSTRICH STEAKS
WITH CHILLI SAUCE AND FIGS

Although ostriches are often associated with South Africa, they were actually introduced by farmers to the south-western part of the country. Before they were hunted out during the nineteenth century, these impressive birds were indigenous in many parts of the continent. Today they still range freely on the plains of East Africa and a few are to be found in south-eastern Egypt.

6 ostrich steaks
black pepper
3 Tbsp butter
2 medium onions, chopped
2 cloves garlic, crushed
2 fresh green chillies, chopped
2 tsp crushed black peppercorns
100 ml red wine
200 ml fresh cream
8 tsp fig jam
salt
6 fresh figs, quartered lengthways

Season the steaks with black pepper. Heat the butter in a frying pan and fry the steaks for 4 minutes on each side, then remove from the pan, but keep warm.

In the same frying pan, sauté the onions, garlic, chillies and peppercorns over a low heat for 5 minutes. Add the wine, cream and jam and boil for 2 minutes. Season with salt.

Arrange the steaks on a serving dish, pour the sauce over and garnish with the figs.

Serve with North African Couscous Salad (see page 134).
SERVES 4–6

GRILLED OSTRICH STEAKS
WITH GOOSEBERRY SAUCE

Because gooseberries are easy to cultivate they are a popular choice for jams and sauces in African cuisine.

4–6 ostrich steaks
2 Tbsp crushed black peppercorns
vegetable oil for grilling

SAUCE
50 g butter
1 onion, chopped
1 Tbsp cake flour
½ cup white wine
1 cup chicken stock
½ cup balsamic vinegar
1½ cups gooseberries
salt and pepper

Pat the steaks dry and rub the crushed peppercorns into them. Heat a cast-iron griller, brush the steaks with vegetable oil and grill for 4 minutes on each side. Keep warm.

Heat the butter in a saucepan and sauté the onion until soft. Stir in the flour until it starts to brown. Pour in the white wine, stirring all the time, then add the chicken stock and simmer for a few minutes. Stir in the vinegar and gooseberries and season with salt and pepper.

Arrange the ostrich steaks on a serving dish, pour over the sauce and serve with Sweet Potato and Butternut Mash (see page 150). **SERVES 4–6**

Grilled ostrich steaks with gooseberry sauce, and Sweet potato and butternut mash (page 150)

ROAST GUINEA FOWL

Guinea fowl are prolific throughout Africa and their culinary use can be traced back to the diet of the ancient Egyptians. Because the birds breed in such great numbers, they present a ready supply of food.

3 Tbsp vegetable oil
6 guinea fowl breasts, with wings on
½ cup white wine
2 cups cream
2 large sprigs rosemary
salt and pepper
½ cup toasted cashew nuts

Preheat the oven to 200 °C.
Heat the oil in a frying pan, then sear the breasts for 2 minutes on each side. Remove the breasts from the pan and cut off the wings. Discard most of the fat from the pan, but leave about 1 tablespoon, then deglaze with the wine and cream. Add the rosemary, salt and pepper and reduce the heat. Simmer until slightly thick.
Put the breasts and wings into a medium-sized roasting pan, pour over the deglazed sauce and bake, uncovered, for 20 minutes.
Serve with mashed potatoes and blanched spinach. Arrange the spinach on a serving dish, slice the guinea fowl and place the slices on top of the spinach. Place the wings on top of the breasts, spoon the sauce over and sprinkle with the cashew nuts. **SERVES 4–6**

BRAISED DUCK WITH ORANGE AND LIME SAUCE

Van der Hum® is a South African tangerine-based liqueur. This is duck and orange sauce with a twist!

2 kg duck, cut into portions
salt and pepper
3 Tbsp cake flour
4 Tbsp olive oil
50 ml chicken stock
100 ml Van der Hum® liqueur or medium sherry
1 cup orange juice
150 ml lime or lemon juice
chopped fresh parsley to garnish

Preheat the oven to 180 °C.
Season the duck with the salt and pepper and dust with the flour. Heat the oil in a frying pan and brown the duck portions. Pour in the stock, liqueur or sherry, orange juice and lime or lemon juice. Transfer all to an ovenproof dish and roast, covered, in the oven for 1 hour. Garnish with the parsley.
Serve with Baked Cabbage with Bacon and Potato (see page 145). **SERVES 4–6**

ROAST DUCK

Duck is a delicacy in Africa and in central Africa it is traditional to serve roast duck to important guests or when your son-in-law is coming to dinner!

6 duck breasts
1 onion, chopped
6 Tbsp vegetable oil
2 Tbsp grated fresh ginger
½ cup water
5 Tbsp soy sauce
1 Tbsp brown sugar
vegetable oil for frying
salt and pepper

Preheat the oven to 200 °C.

Using a sharp knife, score a criss-cross pattern across the skin of the duck breasts. Mix together the onion, 6 tablespoons oil, ginger, water, soy sauce and brown sugar, and marinate the duck breasts in the mixture for 30 minutes. Remove from the marinade and pat dry.

Heat the oil in a frying pan and fry the breasts, skin-side down, for 5 minutes. Transfer to a roasting pan and roast in the oven for 15 minutes.

Discard the fat from the frying pan, add the marinade and simmer, covered, for 5 minutes. Season with the salt and pepper and serve as a sauce over the duck.

Serve with Sweet Potato and Butternut Mash (see page 150).

SERVES 4–6

DUCK BREAST WITH GRILLED NECTARINES AND RED WINE SAUCE

By grilling the nectarines their natural sugars caramelise, creating a colourful garnish for this dish. The nectarines also combine well with the red wine sauce. If nectarines are out of season, substitute them with sliced pineapple rings.

6 duck breasts
salt and pepper
2 Tbsp olive oil
6 nectarines, stoned and halved

SAUCE
2 Tbsp butter
1 Tbsp cake flour
300 ml red wine
1 cup chicken stock
salt

Preheat the grill.

Pat the duck breasts dry and season to taste with the salt and pepper. Heat the oil in a frying pan and fry approximately 6 minutes per side until brown, beginning with the skin sides. Remove from the frying pan and keep warm.

Grill the nectarines, skin-side down, until light brown. Set aside with the duck.

In the same pan in which the duck was fried, discard all the fat, add the butter and stir in the flour until it starts to brown. Pour in the wine and whisk to prevent lumps from forming. Pour in the chicken stock and simmer until slightly reduced. Season with the salt.

Arrange the duck breasts on a serving dish, pour the wine sauce over and top with the grilled nectarines. Serve with mashed potatoes. **SERVES 4–6**

DUCK BREAST WITH GREEN OLIVES
AND AMARULA® SAUCE

Amarula® liqueur with its strawberry-like aroma warrants a special mention. The fruit used is the berry of the marula tree and these berries are a favourite with elephants in the wild. The berries are also used in home brews in Africa.

6 duck breasts

salt and pepper

2 Tbsp vegetable oil

1 cup chicken stock

2 Tbsp brandy

¼ cup Amarula® liqueur

½ cup pitted green olives, halved

½ cup sour cream

Pat the duck breasts dry, then score the skin in a criss-cross pattern
with a sharp knife. Season the breasts with the salt and pepper.
Heat the oil in a frying pan and brown the breasts for 5 minutes on each side.
Remove from the pan and keep warm.
Pour off most of the fat from the frying pan, leaving
2 tablespoons of oil. Pour in the chicken stock and boil for
5 minutes. Lower the heat and add the brandy, liqueur and olives. Stir well,
then add the sour cream and heat for 1 minute. Season with salt and pepper.
Slice the duck, arrange on a serving plate and pour the sauce over the slices.
Serve with Baked Sweet Potatoes Stuffed with Vegetables (see page 113).

SERVES 4–6

MEAT

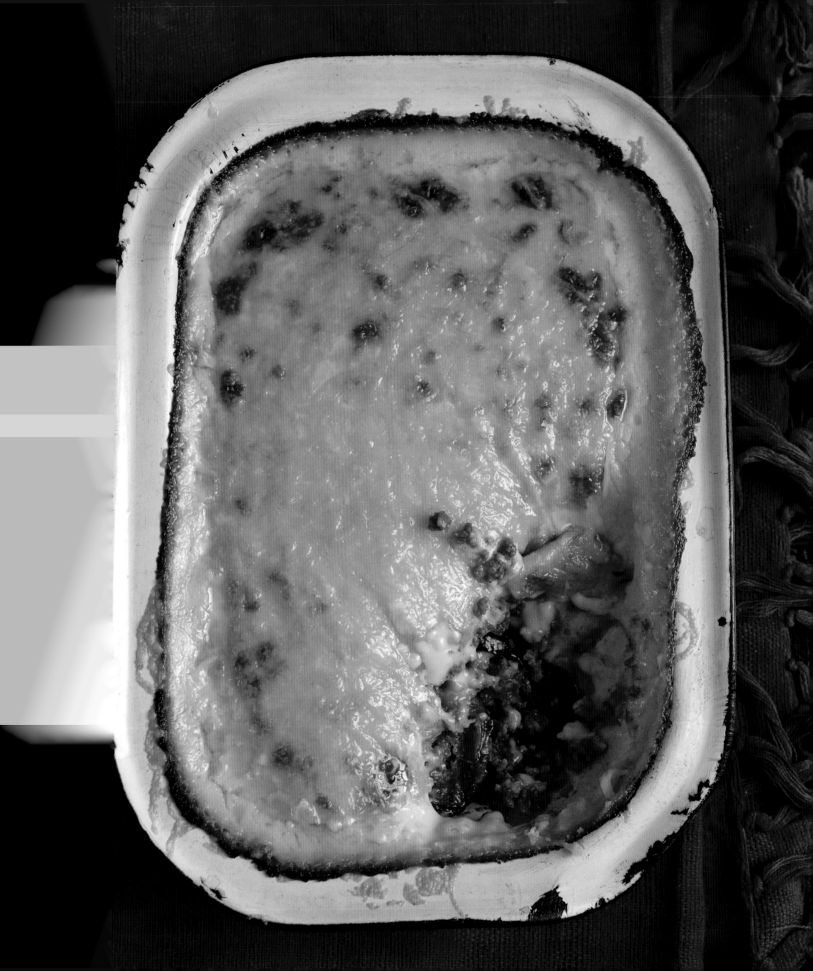

MOUSSAKA

Contrary to popular belief, moussaka isn't a purely Greek dish. It appears that the word itself is of Persian-Arabic origin, i.e. magouma which in Arabic means 'soaked' and in Persian means 'a dish of many layers' including minced lamb, brinjal and onion. There are endless variations across the Middle East and it is from there, via the Mediterranean, that it found its way to Africa.

1 kg brinjals, sliced
salt and pepper
4 Tbsp olive oil
2 onions, finely chopped
2 cloves garlic, crushed
500 g minced beef
1 x 410 g can peeled tomatoes
½ tsp ground cloves
1 tsp ground cinnamon
grated cheddar cheese for sprinkling

CHEESE SAUCE
60 g butter
60 g cake flour
600 ml milk
100 g cheddar cheese, grated
salt and pepper

Preheat the oven to 200 °C. Grease a large ovenproof dish. Place the brinjal slices in a colander and sprinkle them with the salt. Set aside to drain for 1 hour, then rinse thoroughly in cold water and pat dry. Sprinkle the slices with a little of the olive oil and fry in a frying pan for 1 minute on each side, then set aside.

Heat the remaining oil in a pot and fry the onions for 5 minutes over a low heat, add the garlic and beef mince and fry until light brown. Finally, add the tomatoes, cloves, cinnamon and season with salt and pepper. Cook for 5 minutes.

For the sauce, melt the butter in a saucepan and stir in the flour. Add the milk and keep stirring until the sauce is smooth. Add the cheese and stir until it has completely melted, then season with salt and pepper.

Arrange a layer of brinjal in the prepared dish, followed by a layer of mince. Repeat. Pour over the cheese sauce and sprinkle with the grated cheese. Bake for 45 minutes.

Serve with Three-Bean Salad with Olives (see page 139).

SERVES 4–6

LAMB AND BRINJAL STEW

This highly popular North African dish creates its own, delicious gravy. Lamb neck is a good cut to use as it is ideal for the low heat and lengthy cooking time required.

4 Tbsp vegetable oil
500 g stewing lamb (e.g. neck)
3 onions, chopped
2 cloves garlic, crushed
2 x 410 g cans peeled tomatoes
1 Tbsp tomato paste
1 tsp dried thyme
1 litre chicken stock
1 large brinjal, cubed
salt and pepper

Heat the oil in a large saucepan and brown the lamb in batches. Remove from the pan and set aside.
In the same pan, sauté the onions until soft, and add the garlic, tomatoes, tomato paste and thyme. Cook, uncovered, for 5 minutes then pour in the chicken stock and add the lamb. Simmer for 50–60 minutes. Stir in the brinjal cubes and simmer for a further 10 minutes, or until cooked. Season to taste.
Serve with Savoury Rice (see page 133). **SERVES 4–6**

LAMB SHANKS WITH BABY ONIONS, BRINJALS AND PEPPERS

This is a really flavourful lamb dish of West African origin and the perfect meal for a winter evening. Be sure to cook lamb shanks slowly.

6 lamb shanks
1 cup seasoned cake flour (i.e. with salt and pepper)
¼ cup olive oil
1 red pepper, diced
1 yellow pepper, diced
1 green pepper, diced
36 whole baby onions
1 x 410 g can peeled tomatoes
1 brinjal, cubed
1 cup white wine
2 cups chicken stock
salt and pepper

Preheat the oven 175 °C.
Dust the lamb shanks with the seasoned flour and fry in the olive oil until brown.
Transfer the shanks to an ovenproof dish. Arrange all the vegetables over the shanks. Combine the wine and chicken stock and pour over the shanks and vegetables. Season to taste. Cover the dish and roast for 1–1¼ hours.
Serve with rice. **SERVES 4–6**

Lamb shanks with baby onions, brinjals and peppers

LAMB SAUSAGES WRAPPED WITH BACON

If you'd like to serve these as snacks instead of a main course, use cocktail sausages wrapped with half a bacon rasher each.

12 rashers streaky bacon
12 lamb or beef sausages

Wrap a bacon rasher around each sausage and fasten with a toothpick. Place under the grill of an oven (or over hot coals), turning regularly until they are brown. Serve with Sweet Potato and Butternut Mash (see page 150). **SERVES 4–6**

LAMB KIDNEYS

It is traditional in Africa to soak raw kidneys in cold water for 30 minutes before cooking, to remove their distinctive odour. This dish is perfect for breakfast or brunch.

2 Tbsp vegetable oil
1 onion, roughly chopped
2 cloves garlic, peeled
1 fresh green chilli, finely chopped
12 lamb kidneys, thin layer and white membrane removed
100 ml white wine
100 ml chicken stock
1 Tbsp cream cheese
salt and pepper

Heat the oil in a frying pan and sauté the onion until soft. Add the garlic and chilli and stir-fry for 2 minutes, then add the kidneys and cook for 3 minutes. Pour in the wine and when it starts to boil, add the chicken stock and cream cheese. Season with salt and pepper. Serve with mashed potatoes. **SERVES 4–6**

Lamb sausages wrapped with bacon

MOROCCAN LAMB TAGINE

Tagine dishes are really slow-cooked stews, usually made with mutton, or lamb, which is even more tender and therefore cuts down on cooking time. This is a well-known Moroccan recipe; the stew is braised at a low temperature to ensure extra tender meat while the aromatic vegetables are characterised by a spicy sauce. Tunisian cuisine also offers tagines, but those are more akin to Italian frittatas.

12 lamb chops
salt and pepper
4 Tbsp olive oil
2 onions, chopped
3 carrots, peeled and thickly sliced
3 cloves garlic, crushed
2 tsp turmeric
¼ tsp ground cinnamon
¼ tsp ground ginger
4 tsp chopped coriander leaves
2 cups beef stock
12 pitted prunes
¼ cup pine nuts, toasted

Season the chops with the salt and pepper. Heat the oil in a tagine or casserole dish and brown the chops on both sides on the stove top. Add the onions, carrots and garlic, and sauté for 3 minutes.
Add the turmeric, cinnamon, ginger and coriander leaves and stir to combine. Pour in the stock and adjust the seasoning.
Simmer for 1 hour, but add the prunes 10 minutes before the end of cooking time.
Transfer to a serving dish and sprinkle the pine nuts on top. Serve with rice or couscous. **SERVES 4–6**

ROAST LEG OF LAMB WITH BRINJALS

Salting the cubed brinjals and leaving them to 'weep' for a few minutes before cooking eliminates their naturally bitter taste, but rinse them well afterwards so that most of the salt is removed. Harissa paste is a hot red chilli paste.

2 kg leg of lamb
salt and pepper
¼ cup olive oil
4 red onions, cut into wedges
6 cloves garlic, chopped
1 x 410 g can peeled tomatoes
1 cup beef stock
1 Tbsp Harissa Hot Chilli Paste (see page 153)
1 tsp dried thyme
½ tsp chopped fresh mint
3 brinjals, cubed

Preheat the oven to 160 °C.
Put the meat into a deep roasting pan and season with the salt and pepper.
In a bowl, mix together the olive oil, onions, garlic, tomatoes, beef stock, harissa paste, thyme, mint and salt and pepper. Pour the mixture over the meat. Cover securely with foil and roast for 45 minutes. Add the brinjals, cover again and roast for a further 45 minutes.
Baste the meat with the pan juices and roast, uncovered, for another 15 minutes, by which time the meat should be tender.
Serve with Garlic Potatoes (see page 153) and bread to soak up the sauce. **SERVES 4–6**

SPICED LAMB CHOPS

It is traditional for many Africans to display their wealth by the quantity of livestock they own. When a man plans to marry he has to work hard to purchase sufficient livestock to be slaughtered during the wedding ceremony. Lamb is often used for this purpose and the meat is prepared in a variety of ways.

3 Tbsp olive oil
1 onion, chopped
3 cloves garlic, crushed
1 tsp soy sauce
1 fresh green chilli, chopped
¼ cup red wine vinegar
2 Tbsp balsamic vinegar
½ cup red wine
2 cups beef stock (from 1 stock cube)
salt and pepper
12 lamb chops

Heat the oil in a frying pan, then sauté the onion for 5 minutes. Add the garlic, soy sauce, chilli, red wine vinegar and balsamic vinegar, then simmer, covered, for 3 minutes. Pour in the red wine and cook for an additional 3 minutes. Add the beef stock and cook for 10–15 minutes over a low heat. Season with the salt and pepper. Leave to cool.
Marinate the chops in the sauce overnight.
The following day, prepare a charcoal fire. Braai the chops over the coals for approximately 10 minutues, basting regularly with the leftover marinade.
Serve the chops with roast potatoes and a salad of your choice.
SERVES 4–6

LAMB CURRY

This is a simplified version of Zanzibar's beef curry, which is called M'chuzi wanyama.

6 Tbsp olive oil
1 kg lamb, cubed
3 onions, chopped
4 cloves garlic, crushed
2 Tbsp medium curry powder
1 tsp turmeric
½ tsp garam masala
¼ tsp cayenne pepper
4 fresh tomatoes, peeled and chopped
1 chicken stock cube, dissolved in 3 cups boiling water
salt and freshly ground pepper

In a frying pan, heat 4 tablespoons of the oil and brown the meat in batches. Transfer the lamb to a stovetop casserole dish. Add the remaining oil to the same frying pan and sauté the onions and garlic until soft. Stir in the curry powder, turmeric, garam masala and cayenne pepper and fry for 5 minutes. Add the tomatoes and cook until soft, then pour in the chicken stock and boil for 3 minutes. Remove from the heat. Once cool, blend until smooth and pour over the lamb. Cover the dish and leave to simmer gently until the meat is tender – about 1 hour. Serve with basmati rice. **SERVES 4–6**

MUTTON WITH SWEETCORN AND BEANS

Meat, maize and beans represent the staple diet in many African countries. This is a traditional recipe combining all three.

3 Tbsp vegetable oil
500 g mutton, cubed
2 large onions, chopped
2 cloves garlic, crushed
1 tsp dried thyme
1 tsp turmeric
1 tsp dried rosemary
1 tsp cayenne pepper
1 Tbsp tomato paste
4 cups chicken stock
1 cup cooked sweetcorn or canned sweetcorn
1 x 410 g can red or white beans, drained
salt and pepper

Heat the oil in a large frying pan and lightly brown the mutton. Add the onions and garlic and fry until soft, then stir in the thyme, turmeric, rosemary, cayenne pepper and tomato paste. Fry together for 3 minutes then pour in the stock. Simmer gently for 1 hour. Add the sweetcorn and beans and simmer for a further 10 minutes.
Serve with rice. **SERVES 4–6**

BEEF AND VEGETABLE PIE

4 Tbsp vegetable oil
500 g stewing steak, cubed
1 large onion, chopped
1 stick celery
¼ cup red wine
2 cups beef stock
2 carrots, peeled and sliced
250 g button mushrooms, sliced
½ cup each shelled peas and fresh cream
2 Tbsp cake flour
salt and pepper
1 egg yolk, beaten

PASTRY
250 g cake flour
½ tsp salt
150 g butter, cut into pieces
180 ml cold water
1 tsp lemon juice
1 egg yolk

In a large pot, heat the oil and brown the meat. Add the onion and celery and sauté until soft. Pour in the wine and beef stock and simmer for 1 hour. Stir in the carrots, mushrooms and peas. Mix the cream into the flour, add to the meat and season to taste. Simmer for 10 minutes until the sauce thickens. Leave to cool.
Grease a pie dish and preheat the oven to 180 °C. For the pastry, sift the flour and salt into a bowl and rub in the butter until the mixture resembles fine breadcrumbs. Beat together the water, lemon juice and egg yolk then mix with the flour until a dough forms. Roll out half of the pastry and line the pie dish.
Spoon the cooled filling into the pie dish and cover with the rest of the pastry. Brush with the beaten egg yolk and bake for 30 minutes. **SERVES 4–6**

BOBOTIE

This is a traditional South African dish made with minced beef or lamb. However, minced chicken may also be used as a healthy and delicious alternative. Of Cape Malay origin, bobotie has a spicy, fruity taste with just a hint of curry.

3 Tbsp butter
2 onions, finely chopped
1 stick celery, finely chopped
3 cloves garlic, crushed
500 g minced beef
1 carrot, peeled and finely chopped
¼ cup raisins
1 Tbsp mild curry powder
1 tsp turmeric
½ tsp ground cinnamon
¼ tsp ground cloves
1 large pinch cayenne pepper
½ tsp sugar, dissolved in 2 Tbsp white vinegar
salt and pepper

TOPPING
1 cup double cream
2 eggs
salt and pepper

Preheat the oven to 160 °C. Grease a deep, ovenproof dish. In a pot, heat the butter and sauté the onions and celery until soft. Add the garlic and beef, and stir-fry with a fork to separate the mince. Add the rest of the ingredients (except the salt and pepper) and fry until well combined, then season with the salt and pepper. Spoon the mixture into the ovenproof dish and press gently, levelling the top with the back of a spoon.
Beat together all the topping ingredients lightly with a fork, then pour over the bobotie. Bake for 30 minutes.
Serve with rice. **SERVES 4–6**

Bobotie

BEEF POT ROAST

Traditionally, African people had no access to modern ovens (and many still don't), so pot-roasting is an effective alternative method for roasting meat.

1 Tbsp olive oil
125 g butter
2 kg topside beef roast
4 medium carrots, peeled and chopped
2 large potatoes, chopped
1 large onion, sliced
3 medium leeks, chopped
¼ cup cake flour
½ cup dry red wine
1 litre beef stock
¼ cup tomato paste
¼ cup Worcestershire sauce

In a large pan, heat the oil and 20 g of the butter, add the beef and brown all over. Set the meat aside in a large pot.
In the same pan, heat another 20 g of the butter and then add the carrots, potatoes, onion and leeks and cook until browned and softening. Set the vegetables aside.
In the same pan, heat the remaining butter, add the flour and stir until light brown. Remove the pan from the heat and gradually stir in the wine and stock. Return the pan to the heat and continue stirring until the sauce thickens.
Add the sauce and any remaining juices to the pot with the meat, add the tomato paste and Worcestershire sauce and simmer, covered, for about 2 hours or until the beef is tender, turning it occasionally. Add the vegetables that were set aside for the final 20 minutes of cooking, to simmer with the beef.
Serve with Special Cornmeal Bread (see page 166), which is delicious with the gravy, and Green Bean and Tomato Salad (see page 134). **SERVES 4–6**

Beef pot roast

BEEF STEW AND PAP

This is a favourite African stew which is sure to impress most people. It is easy to cook, whether at home or at a bus terminal! Generally stewing or goulash steak is used, but for a tastier and more tender cut, rump may be substituted and the cooking time be reduced accordingly.

¼ cup olive oil
1 onion, roughly chopped
1 kg beef stewing steak or goulash
½ cup red wine
2 cups beef stock
1 Tbsp tomato paste
5 carrots, peeled and sliced 2 cm thick
8 baby onions, peeled and diced
2 potatoes, peeled and cubed
salt and pepper
mealiepap to serve

Heat the oil in a large pot and sauté the onion until soft. Add the beef and brown lightly. Pour in the wine, beef stock and tomato paste. Stir gently until the paste has dissolved, then simmer over a low heat for 40 minutes.
Add the carrots and baby onions and simmer for 15 minutes.
Add the potatoes and simmer for another 7 minutes, or until the potatoes are cooked but still firm. Season to taste with the salt and pepper.
Serve with the mealiepap. **SERVES 4–6**

SPICED BEEF FILLET

In ancient Egypt this dish was reserved for the pharaohs. Luckily we can all enjoy it today. Tahini is a paste of hulled, lightly roasted sesame seeds, popular in Middle Eastern cooking.

1 Tbsp black peppercorns, crushed
1 Tbsp mustard seeds
1 Tbsp coriander seeds, crushed
500 g beef fillet
3 Tbsp butter

SAUCE
¼ cup tahini
1 cup plain yoghurt
juice of 1 lemon
2 Tbsp chopped fresh coriander
¼ tsp cayenne pepper

Preheat the oven to 200 °C.
Mix together the peppercorns, mustard and coriander seeds, then coat the fillet with the mixture.
Heat the butter in a frying pan, sear the meat on all sides, then transfer to a roasting pan and roast for 15 minutes. Leave the meat to rest for 10 minutes before slicing.
In the meanwhile, make the sauce. Gently mix all the ingredients until smooth, then transfer the sauce to a bowl.
Slice the meat thinly and arrange on a platter. Serve with the sauce, roasted vegetables, baked jacket potatoes and Cucumber and Baby Marrow Salad (see page 135). **SERVES 4–6**

OXTAIL STEW WITH MEALIEPAP

Mealiepap gives this tasty dish it's truly African flavour. No self-respecting African oxtail stew is served without it!

1 kg oxtail, cut into joints
cake flour for dusting
5 Tbsp vegetable oil
5 onions, roughly chopped
1 clove garlic, crushed
2 cups beef stock
2 cups red wine
2 bay leaves
3 black peppercorns
1 x 410 g can red beans or dried red beans, cooked
salt and pepper

Dust the oxtail with the flour and heat the oil in a pan. Fry the meat on both sides until brown, then transfer to a large pot. Fry the onions and garlic in the same pan for 5 minutes, then add the mixture to the oxtail. Pour the beef stock and wine over the oxtail, add the bay leaves and peppercorns, and simmer gently, covered, for 3 hours.
Add the beans to the pot, season with the salt and pepper, and leave to simmer for another 10 minutes.
Serve with Mealiepap with Onion and Tomato Sauce (see page 141). **SERVES 4–6**

OX LIVER, ONIONS AND MUSHROOMS

Lamb livers may be substituted for ox livers.

700 g ox liver, sliced into 6
salt and pepper
2 Tbsp butter
3 Tbsp vegetable oil
3 onions, thinly sliced
2 cups sliced button mushrooms
¼ cup white wine
¼ cup sherry
¼ cup fresh cream
1 tsp dried thyme
2 tsp butter

Pat the liver slices dry and season them with the salt and pepper. In a frying pan, heat the butter and 2 tablespoons of the oil and fry the liver quickly on both sides, in batches depending on the size of the frying pan. Keep warm.
In another frying pan, fry the onions in the remaining tablespoon of oil until brown. Add the mushrooms and then stir-fry for 2–5 minutes. Season with salt and pepper, then pile the mushrooms on top of the slices of liver.
Pour the wine and sherry in the frying pan in which the mushrooms were fried and bring to the boil, then stir in the cream and thyme and beat in the 2 teaspoons of butter. Season to taste with salt and pepper.
Arrange the livers and mushrooms in a serving dish and pour over the sauce.
Serve with mashed potatoes. **SERVES 4–6**

Oxtail stew with mealiepap

TONGUE WITH CHICKPEA AND MUSTARD SAUCE

Tongue may not be everyone's favourite, but if cooked correctly can be extremely tasty and tender. It is popular throughout Africa because it is one of the cheapest cuts of meat.

1 ox tongue
2 whole onions, peeled
2 sticks celery, halved
1 carrot
1 leek
8 cups water

SAUCE
100 g butter
4 Tbsp Dijon mustard
¾ cup chicken stock
3 Tbsp white wine
1 tsp cornflour
1 x 410 g can chickpeas, drained
salt

In a pot, simmer the tongue together with the rest of the ingredients for 2 hours until tender, but not overcooked.
In the meanwhile, make the sauce. Melt the butter in a saucepan and stir in the mustard, chicken stock, wine and cornflour. Simmer for 5 minutes. Add the chickpeas and simmer for another 5 minutes, then season with the salt.
Remove the skin from the tongue before slicing it. Arrange the slices in a serving dish and pour the sauce over the tongue.
Serve with Three-Bean Salad with Olives (see page 139). **SERVES 4–6**

SUYA

Very popular in West Africa, suya originated with the Hausa people in northern Nigeria and Niger. It is a form of shish kebab and has proved to be a favourite evening snack sold by many roadside vendors and restaurants. The kebabs can be grilled in the oven or over coals on a charcoal braai. Bamboo skewers burn easily, so wrap both ends in foil or soak them in water for 30 minutes before using.

1 kg minced beef
½ cup roasted peanuts, finely chopped
¼ tsp chilli powder
1 onion, grated
1 tsp ground ginger
1 cup fresh breadcrumbs
salt and pepper
6 bamboo skewers
olive oil

Preheat the grill.
In a bowl, combine the beef and the other ingredients and shape into approximately 24 meatballs. Thread the meatballs onto the bamboo skewers.
Grill for about 10 minutes, then brush with the olive oil.
Serve with Harissa Hot Chilli Paste (see page 153). **SERVES 4–6**

Suya, with Harissa hot chilli paste (page 153)

J'S STEAK

It took me a while to perfect the sauce for this recipe, but as everyone enjoys it, it was worth the effort!

6 beef steaks

SAUCE
3 Tbsp butter
2 onions, roughly chopped
3 cloves garlic, crushed
3 tomatoes, peeled and chopped
½ cup beef stock
½ cup tomato sauce
½ cup J's Spiced Fruit Chutney (see page 154)
2 Tbsp sugar
6 Tbsp red wine vinegar
1 fresh green chilli, finely chopped
3 Tbsp Worcestershire sauce

Heat the butter in a pan. Sauté the onions for 5 minutes. Add the rest of the sauce ingredients and simmer for 5 minutes. Keep warm.
Grill the steaks (4 minutes for rare, 5 minutes for medium and 6 minutes for well done), then spoon the sauce over them.
Serve with Sweet Potato and Butternut Mash (see page 150), Malawi's Favourite Cabbage Salad (see page 135) and J's Spiced Fruit Chutney (see page 154). **SERVES 4–6**

CURRIED RUMP STEAK WITH CHILLI ONION RINGS

Indian settlers, particularly in East Africa and South Africa, introduced the use of curries and spices into African cooking.

5 rump steaks
3 Tbsp butter

MARINADE
2 Tbsp medium curry powder
4 Tbsp olive or vegetable oil
2 Tbsp grated fresh ginger
4 Tbsp soy sauce

ONION RINGS
300 g cake flour (plus extra for dusting)
2 tsp chilli powder
½ tsp salt
2 tsp ground cumin
1 fresh green chilli, deseeded and finely chopped
¼–½ cup water
3 onions, sliced ino 2 mm-thick rings
± 4 cups vegetable oil for deep-frying

Mix together all the marinade ingredients and marinate the steaks for 1 hour. In the meanwhile, for the onion rings mix together the flour, chilli powder, salt, cumin, green chilli and water to make a batter with a thick, dropping consistency. Dust the onion rings with flour and dip them into the batter. In a deep frying pan, heat the vegetable oil and then fry the onion rings until golden brown. Remove the steaks from the marinade, pat them dry and reserve the marinade. Heat the butter in a frying pan and brown the steaks on both sides, about 4 minutes per side. Heat the marinade in a saucepan for 1 minute and pour into a serving dish. Add the steaks to the dish and arrange the onion rings on top. Serve with Sweet Potato Chips (see page 150). **SERVES 4–6**

PAP AND BOEREWORS WITH TOMATO AND ONION SAUCE

This is one of South Africa's favourite dishes and is usually enjoyed at weekend braais. Although the wors *(or farmer's sausage) is grilled on the braai, it can be pan-fried if you prefer.* Pap *is the shortened form of mealiepap (maize meal). This is a simple yet tasty dish.*

6 cups water
3 cups mealie meal
1 tsp salt
1–2 kg boerewors

TOMATO AND ONION SAUCE
4 Tbsp vegetable oil
3 onions, finely chopped
9 tomatoes, peeled and chopped
1 Tbsp tomato paste
1 beef stock cube
½ cup water
salt and pepper

To make the sauce, heat the oil in a pot and sauté the onions for 10 minutes, or until soft. Add the tomatoes and tomato paste and stir over medium heat until the tomatoes are very soft. Stir in the beef stock and water until the cube has dissolved totally, then simmer for 15 minutes. Season with the salt and pepper, but be careful as the beef stock is already very salty.

For the mealiepap, bring the water to a boil in a large pot. Sprinkle in the maize meal, little by little, stirring continuously with a wooden spoon until thick. Reduce the heat, season with salt and cook, covered, for 15 minutes.

In the meanwhile, grill the boerewors for approximately 10 minutes, or until done. Serve the boerewors with the pap and sauce. **SERVES 4–6**

BOEREWORS AND PINEAPPLE KEBABS WITH ONION MARMALADE

The contrasting yet complementary flavours in this dish create an unusual taste experience.

1 kg boerewors, cut into 2 cm-thick slices
2 large pineapples, peeled and cubed
2 onions, cut into wedges
6 bamboo skewers (see page 69)
vegetable oil

ONION MARMALADE
3 Tbsp vegetable oil
5 onions, sliced into rings
2 tsp brown sugar
¼ cup balsamic vinegar
a pinch of cayenne pepper

To make the onion marmalade, heat the oil in a frying pan. Add the onions and fry until light brown in colour. Add the sugar and balsamic vinegar, stirring until the onions are coated with the vinegar. Season with the cayenne pepper.

Thread the boerewors slices, pineapple cubes and onion wedges onto the skewers, alternating onion, boerewors, pineapple, boerewors. Brush each kebab with the vegetable oil.

Heat a griddle and cook the kebabs.

Serve the kebabs with the onion marmalade and Sweet Potato and Butternut Mash (see page 150). **SERVES 4–6**

ROAST LOIN OF PORK
IN LEMON CREAM SAUCE

Some African groups do not eat pork for religious reasons. However, in most countries, pork is generally a favourite dish as it is cheaper than beef or lamb. The piquant sauce in this dish adds an interesting touch to a standard roast.

50 ml olive oil
2 kg loin of pork
6 cloves garlic, crushed
2 Tbsp chopped fresh rosemary
2 cups fresh cream
salt and pepper
juice of 1 lemon

Preheat the oven to 180 °C.
Heat the oil in a large frying pan and brown the pork. Transfer the meat to a roasting dish.
Discard the fat from the frying pan, add the garlic and rosemary, and pour in the cream. Season with the salt and pepper. Remove the pan from the heat and quickly stir in the lemon juice.
Pour the cream sauce over the meat in the roasting dish and roast, covered, for 60 minutes, and uncovered for a further 20 minutes. Leave the meat to stand for 10 minutes before carving.
Serve with Roasted Rosemary Potatoes (see page 146).
SERVES 4–6

NIGERIAN MEAT KEBABS

Many Nigerians believe that to create good flavour in food, it is essential to mix different kinds of meat. These kebabs are a good example of this and are a popular addition to the barbecue menu of Nigerian immigrants in other countries.

200 g minced beef
1 onion, finely chopped
1 Tbsp chopped fresh parsley
½ tsp salt
2 Tbsp fresh breadcrumbs
6 bamboo skewers (see page 69)
4 chicken breasts, cubed
4 ostrich steaks, cubed

BASTING SAUCE
½ cup honey
½ cup brown or white vinegar
3 Tbsp Dijon mustard
4 cloves garlic, crushed

In a large bowl, combine the mince, onion, parsley, salt and breadcrumbs and shape into approximately 12 small meatballs. Thread them onto the skewers, alternating with the chicken and ostrich cubes.
Combine all the basting sauce ingredients. Braai the kebabs over the coals for 10 minutes, basting regularly with the sauce.
Serve with Yam Patties (see page 21) and the basting sauce.
SERVES 4–6

Nigerian meat kebabs

ROAST LOIN OF PORK WITH FENNEL BULBS

Dried fennel leaves, as well as the fleshy bulb and seeds, have an anise flavour. Toasting the seeds accentuates their flavour.

6-rib pork loin standing rib roast (± 2 kg), skin scored
1 heaped Tbsp green fennel seeds, finely ground
4 cloves garlic, crushed
2 tsp coarse salt
6 fennel bulbs, halved
6 potatoes, peeled
2 cups beef stock
salt and pepper

APPLE SAUCE
4 apples, peeled and sliced
1 tsp sugar
¼ cup water
2 Tbsp lemon juice

STEAMED SPINACH
2 kg spinach
3 Tbsp olive oil
salt and pepper

Preheat the oven to 200 °C. Mix the fennel seeds, garlic and coarse salt, then rub into the pork skin. Roast the pork, skin-side up, in a roasting dish for 15 minutes. Reduce the heat to 180 °C. Add the fennel bulbs and potatoes to the dish and roast with the pork for 80 minutes, basting regularly with the stock. Season. Bring all the apple sauce ingredients to the boil in a pot. Cook for 5–10 minutes, then purée in a blender until smooth.
Wash the spinach well. Do not dry, but place in salted boiling water for 2 minutes. Drain, add the olive oil and season to taste. Transfer the roast onto a serving platter and carve into chops. Serve with the steamed spinach and apple sauce. **SERVES 4–6**

GAMMON WITH HONEY AND MUSTARD GLAZE

African cuisine has been influenced by Western Christmas traditions and so gammon is a popular addition to the festive table.

2 kg gammon
1 stick celery
2 whole onions, peeled
1 leek
2 carrots, peeled
½ cup chicken stock
2 Tbsp fresh cream

HONEY AND MUSTARD GLAZE
100 ml honey
3 Tbsp wholegrain mustard
3 Tbsp hot English mustard
4 Tbsp white wine

Preheat the oven to 200 °C.
In a large pot, cover the gammon, celery, onions, leek and carrots with water and simmer for 40 minutes.
In the meanwhile, mix together the glaze ingredients.
Transfer the gammon to a roasting pan, score lines into the skin 1 cm apart and brush with the honey and mustard glaze.
Roast for 30 minutes until the skin is shiny and keep basting with the glaze. Leave to rest for 10 minutes.
Make a gravy by heating the pan juices. Add the half cup of chicken stock and bring to the boil. Stir in the cream and pour into a gravy boat.
Serve with Roasted Rosemary Potatoes (see page 146).
SERVES 4–6

Gammon with honey and mustard glaze, and Roasted rosemary potatoes (page 146)

PORK SPARERIBS

All over the world steakhouses vie to see who can produce the best pork spareribs and their success depends on the marinade in question. In Africa it is no different!

1.5–2 kg pork spareribs

MARINADE
100 ml soy sauce
2 onions, finely chopped
1 clove garlic, crushed
1 Tbsp sherry
100 ml red wine vinegar
¾ cup beef stock
salt
100 ml tomato sauce
1 tsp sugar
1 tsp ground ginger
1 tsp ground cloves
50 ml J's Spiced Fruit Chutney (see page 154)

Mix together all the marinade ingredients, then marinate the meat overnight.
Remove the ribs from the marinade and grill, basting regularly with the marinade. The marinade can also be used as a sauce if it is simmered over a low heat for 5–10 minutes.
Serve the ribs with Charmoula Potatoes (see page 149).
SERVES 4–6

ROAST SADDLE OF SPRINGBOK WITH PRUNES AND PORT SAUCE

Springboks are antelopes, of which the largest number are found in the Kalahari. They are known for their running speed and jumping ability and as a result are the emblem for South Africa's national rugby team.

3 Tbsp melted butter
3 Tbsp vegetable oil
2 tsp chopped mixed fresh herbs (e.g. parsley and rosemary)
sea salt and crushed black peppercorns
3 kg saddle of springbok

SAUCE
2 Tbsp butter
2 Tbsp cake flour
150 ml port or medium sherry
400 ml chicken stock
100 g soft dried prunes, pitted

Preheat the oven to 180 °C.
Mix together the butter, oil, herbs and salt and pepper, then rub over the meat. Roast in the oven for 30 minutes.
In the meanwhile, make the sauce. In a saucepan, melt the butter and stir in the flour. Keep stirring until light brown then pour in the port or sherry. Gradually add the chicken stock and keep stirring until there are no lumps. Add the prunes and cook for 15 minutes.
Slice the meat and serve with the sauce, Roasted Rosemary Potatoes (see page 146) and Green Bean and Tomato Salad (see page 134). **SERVES 4–6**

ROAST SADDLE OF SPRINGBOK WITH J'S SPICED FRUIT CHUTNEY

3 kg saddle of springbok
salt and pepper
butter
1 cup J's Spiced Fruit Chutney (see page 154)
2 tsp chopped fresh herbs (e.g. parsley, rosemary, basil)
1 cup water

Preheat the oven to 180 °C.
Season the meat with salt and pepper to taste. Heat a large frying pan and add a knob of butter. Brown the meat all over. Transfer the meat to a roasting pan and spread the chutney over, then sprinkle the herbs on top. Roast in the oven for 30 minutes. Remove the meat and keep warm.
To make a gravy, pour the water into the roasting pan and bring to the boil. Strain and decant into a gravy boat.
Slice the meat and serve with the gravy and Rice Balls Stuffed with Cheese and Basil (see page 110). **SERVES 4–6**

Roast saddle of springbok with J's spiced fruit chutney, and Rice balls stuffed with cheese and basil (page 110)

VENISON KEBABS IN PORT AND ROSEMARY MARINADE

Originally the meat of any animal killed in hunting was called venison. Nowadays, the term refers to the meat of various species of deer.

2 onions, cut into wedges
700 g venison fillet, cubed
4 unripe bananas, peeled and sliced 2-cm thick
6 bamboo skewers (see page 69)

MARINADE
1 onion, finely chopped
2 cloves garlic, crushed
½ tsp crushed black peppercorns
1 Tbsp chopped fresh rosemary
1 cup port
2 Tbsp vegetable oil
3 Tbsp white vinegar
½ cup beef stock
2 Tbsp water

Thread the onion wedges, venison cubes and banana slices alternately onto each skewer. Place the skewers into a dish. Boil together all the marinade ingredients for 5 minutes then leave to cool. Pour over the kebabs and marinate for 1 hour. Grill the kebabs over coals or in a cast-iron griddle pan until cooked to taste, regularly basting with the leftover marinade. Serve with Rice and Sweetcorn Salad (see page 139).
SERVES 4–6

Venison kebabs in port and rosemary marinade, with Rice and sweetcorn salad (page 139)

VENISON AND BACON CASSEROLE

Because venison is low in fat, it is considered to be one of the healthier meats to eat. What fat there is, isn't marbled as it is in beef or pork. Marbling, or animal fat, is the source of cholesterol.

1 kg venison, boned and cut into 1-cm cubes
3 Tbsp olive oil
150 g streaky bacon, diced
2 onions, finely chopped
2 carrots, peeled and sliced
½ cup red wine
2 cups chicken stock
3 bay leaves
salt and pepper
cake flour for dusting
200 g whole button mushrooms

MARINADE
¼ cup olive oil
¼ cup brown vinegar
½ cup red wine
1 onion, cut into wedges
½ tsp dried rosemary

Put the venison in a large bowl. Mix together all the marinade ingredients and pour over the meat. Marinate overnight. Discard the marinade and pat the meat dry.

Heat 1 tablespoon of the oil in a frying pan and fry the bacon until brown. Add the onions and carrots and cook for 5 minutes. Pour in the wine and boil for 2 minutes. Add the chicken stock and bay leaves. Transfer all to a casserole dish.

Season the meat with the salt and pepper and dust with flour. Add the remaining oil to the frying pan and fry the meat in batches, then add to the casserole dish and simmer for 40 minutes. Add the mushrooms and simmer for a further 30 minutes.

Serve with rice and bread to mop up the sauce. **SERVES 4–6**

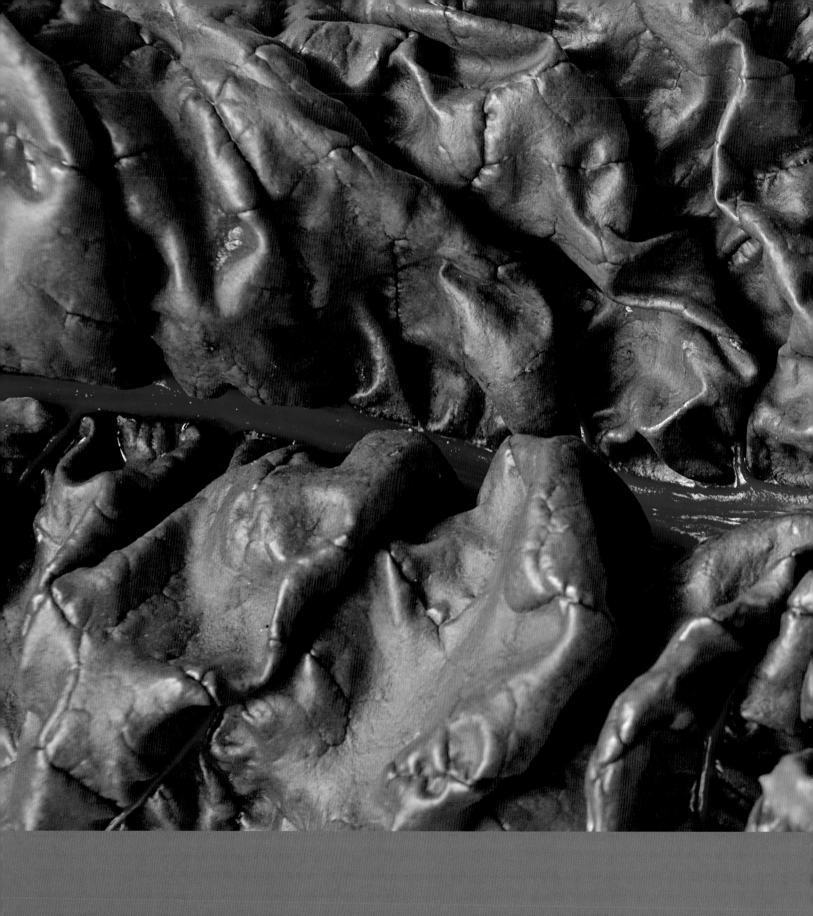

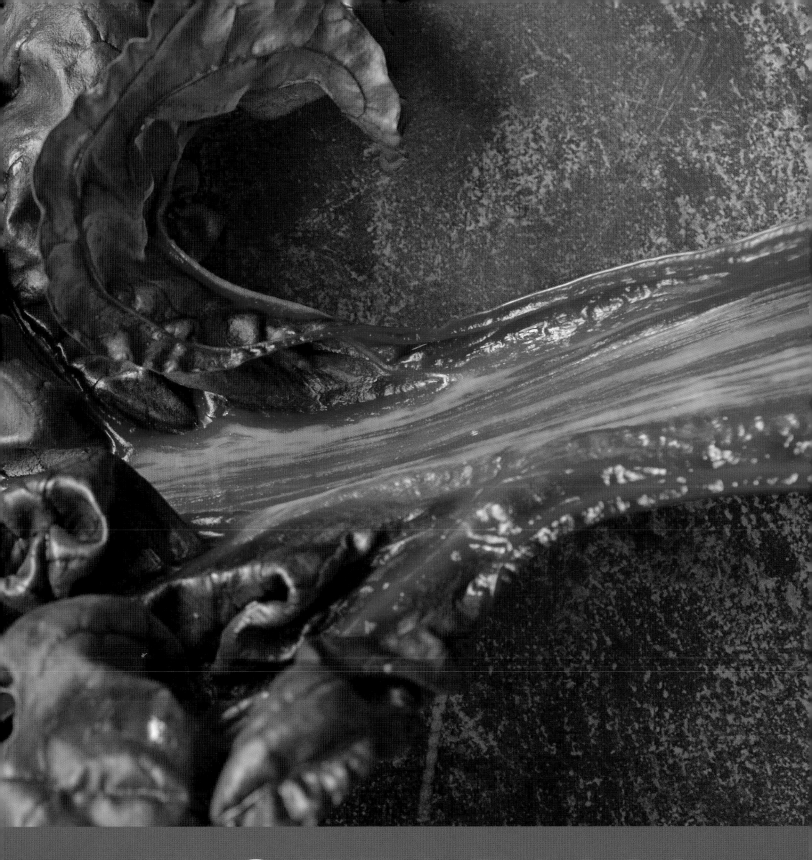

VEGETARIAN

VEGETABLE TART

Many Africans are vegetarian for differing reasons (including religion, affordability and availability). This wholesome tart makes an excellent main meal.

PASTRY
200 g cake flour
100 g butter
1 egg yolk
5 Tbsp water

FILLING
50 g butter
6 spring onions, sliced
1 red onion, sliced
1 red pepper, sliced
200 g broccoli florets
2 medium potatoes, peeled and cubed
100 g butternut, peeled and diced
50 g feta cheese, crumbled
1 cup sour cream
3 egg yolks
salt and pepper
50 g cheddar cheese, grated

Preheat the oven to 180 °C. Grease a 23 cm fluted pie dish. Sift the flour into a bowl and rub in the butter with your fingers until it resembles fine breadcrumbs. Beat together the egg yolk and water, then pour into the flour mixture. Knead the pastry until smooth. Roll out the pastry and line the pie dish with it. Prick the base of the pastry with a fork and bake blind for 10 minutes. For the filling, heat the butter in a saucepan and sauté all the vegetables for 5 minutes. Spoon the mixture into the pastry shell then sprinkle the feta over the top. Beat together the sour cream and egg yolks, salt and pepper and spoon over the vegetables. Top with the grated cheese and bake for 30 minutes. **SERVES 4–6**

RICE BALLS STUFFED WITH CHEESE AND BASIL

Although this is a vegetarian dish, it could also accompany chicken or meat, or be served as a pre-dinner snack.

50 g butter
1 onion, finely chopped
250 g uncooked white glutinous rice (sticky rice)
1 Tbsp tomato paste
3 cups water
1 tsp salt
100 g cheddar cheese or brie, cubed
16 fresh basil leaves
cake flour for coating
1 egg, beaten
cornflake crumbs
1 cup vegetable oil

Heat the butter in a pot and sauté the onion until soft. Add the rice and stir until the grains are coated with butter and onion. Stir in the tomato paste and keep stirring until the rice turns red. Add the water and salt. Stir gently and cook for 15–20 minutes, or until all the water has been absorbed, then leave to cool. Shape the rice mixture into 15–16 balls. Make a hole in each ball with your finger, then stuff with a cube of cheese and a basil leaf. Roll each ball in the flour, then dip into the beaten egg and coat with the cornflake crumbs. Refrigerate for 1 hour. Heat the oil in a pan and fry the rice balls until brown. Serve on a bed of salad. **SERVES 4–6**

Vegetable tart

BAKED SWEET POTATOES STUFFED WITH VEGETABLES

This recipe is from Rwanda, where it is known as ibijumba nibishyimba nimboga. *In Rwanda they normally use* amamesa *(coconut oil) from the Congo, but olive oil is just as suitable.*

3 large sweet potatoes
3 Tbsp butter or olive oil
2 onions, finely chopped
½ tsp cumin seeds
100 g green beans, cooked and diced
150 g shelled peas
2 Tbsp chopped fresh coriander
2 cooked yellow mealies (corn-on-the-cob), kernels removed
salt and a good pinch of cayenne pepper

Preheat the oven to 180 °C, then bake the sweet potatoes for 50–60 minutes, or until soft.
In the meanwhile, melt the butter in a saucepan and sauté the onions until soft. Add the cumin seeds and fry for 2 minutes. Remove the pan from the heat, add the rest of the ingredients and toss. Season with the salt and cayenne pepper. Cut the baked potatoes in half lengthways and scoop out the flesh to mix with the vegetables. Stuff the mixture back into the potato shells and bake for 20 minutes. **SERVES 4–6**

Baked sweet potatoes stuffed with vegetables

BREAD BASKETS WITH MUSHROOMS, TOMATOES AND GOAT'S MILK CHEESE

Because cows are more susceptible to disease in the tropics, goat's milk is often used instead and it makes wonderful cheese. For a non-vegetarian option, you could sprinkle chopped, crispy bacon over the top of the bread baskets before baking.

6 thick slices wholewheat bread, crusts removed
3 Tbsp butter
3 cloves garlic, crushed
220 g white button mushrooms, sliced
¼ cup sour cream
3 firm, ripe tomatoes, peeled, deseeded and chopped
180 g goat's milk cheese, crumbled or diced
1 Tbsp fresh chopped parsley
salt and pepper

Preheat the oven to 200 °C. Grease a 6-cup muffin pan and line each cup with a slice of bread, ensuring that it reaches the bottom. Bake until the bread starts to brown and then remove the pan from the oven but leave the bread in the cups.
In a pan, heat the butter and fry the garlic for 10 seconds. Add the mushrooms and fry until all the moisture has evaporated. Pour in the sour cream and when it starts to boil, remove from the heat. Add the tomatoes, cheese and parsley. Season with the salt and pepper. Spoon the mixture into the bread baskets and bake for 10 minutes.
Serve while hot with Malawi's Favourite Cabbage Salad (see page 135). **SERVES 4–6**

MOROGO WITH PEANUTS AND MUSHROOMS

Women picking out the morogo (wild spinach), growing in between other crops, is a familiar sight in rural South Africa. This dish is as delicious as it is nutritious. If you cannot find morogo, ordinary spinach or Swiss chard may be used as a substitute.

4 Tbsp olive oil
2 onions, finely chopped
4 tomatoes, peeled and chopped
1 cup raw peanuts, soaked in water for 3 hours
1 tsp ground cumin
200 g mushrooms
1 cup vegetable stock
400 g spinach, roughly chopped
salt

In a large pot, heat the oil and sauté the onions until soft. Stir in the tomatoes, peanuts and cumin, and cook for 10 minutes over a low heat. Add the mushrooms and the stock and simmer for another 10 minutes. Add the spinach, but do not cook for longer than 5 minutes after this. Season with the salt. Serve with mealiepap. **SERVES 4–6**

VEGETABLE STEW WITH PEANUT BUTTER

For the rural people of Africa, vegetables add variety and nutrients to a starchy diet comprising mostly maize, cassava, yams, millet and beans, with occasional meat stews.

4 Tbsp olive oil
2 onions, roughly chopped
4 cloves garlic, crushed
½ tsp ground ginger
200 g whole button mushrooms
3 sweet potatoes, peeled and cubed
2 cups vegetable stock
100 g white cabbage, thinly sliced
4 Tbsp peanut butter
salt
¼ tsp cayenne pepper

In a large pot, heat the oil and sauté the onions for about 7 minutes, or until soft. Add the garlic, ginger, mushrooms and potatoes and stir-fry until the vegetables are coated with the spice. Pour in the stock and simmer for 10 minutes. Add the rest of the ingredients and stir until the peanut butter has melted. Simmer for 5 minutes before serving. **SERVES 4–6**

Morogo with peanuts and mushrooms

TOMATO AND BLUE CHEESE TART

Many Southern African boutique and larger cheese manufacturers make high quality, inexpensive blue cheeses.

PASTRY
200 g cake flour
100 g butter
1 egg yolk
3 Tbsp iced water

FILLING
3 Tbsp butter
1 onion, chopped
2 leeks, sliced
4 cloves garlic, crushed
100 g blue cheese
300 g cherry tomatoes, halved
10 g basil leaves, shredded
sea salt and pepper
olive oil to drizzle

Preheat the oven to 200 °C. Grease a 20-cm fluted flan dish. Sift the flour into a bowl and rub in the butter until it resembles breadcrumbs. Beat the yolk with the water, stir it into the flour mixture and knead lightly for 4 minutes until smooth. Chill the pastry for 20 minutes, then roll it out on a floured surface and line the dish. Prick the base with a fork and bake blind for 15 minutes.

For the filling, heat the butter in a pan and sauté the onion, leeks and garlic until soft. Spoon the mixture into the baked pastry shell. Crumble over the blue cheese and arrange the tomatoes on top in a circle in a single layer, starting from the middle, until the pastry shell is filled. Finally, scatter the basil, grind over sea salt and pepper and drizzle with the olive oil. Bake at 180 °C for 20 minutes or until the tomatoes are soft but still whole, and the custard is set.

Serve with a salad. **SERVES 4–6**

BEANS AND MAIZE WITH PEANUTS

In the Kinyarwanda language of Rwanda, this dish is known as ibishyimbo nibigori *and is very popular in that country. Samp and beans form the staple diet for many people throughout Africa.*

2 cups dried red beans
2 cups samp
4 cups vegetable stock
4 Tbsp olive oil
2 large onions, roughly chopped
1 tsp turmeric
1 x 410 g can peeled tomatoes
100 g roasted peanuts
salt

Wash the beans and samp and soak in water overnight. Bring them to the boil in a large pot with the vegetable stock. Simmer for 1 hour.

In a saucepan, heat the oil and sauté the onions until soft.

Add the turmeric and fry for 3 minutes, then add the tomatoes and simmer for 15 minutes. Spoon the sauce into the beans and samp, and simmer for 1 hour. Lastly, stir in the peanuts, season with the salt and serve. **SERVES 4–6**

Beans and maize with peanuts

LENTIL DHAL WITH VEGETABLES

Although dhal has its origins in India, it has long been embraced by African cooks, each developing his or her own adaptation. I'm particularly proud of my own version.

3 Tbsp olive oil
1 large onion, finely chopped
1 clove garlic, crushed
1 tsp ground cumin
1 tsp turmeric
¼ tsp cayenne pepper
2 cups brown lentils, washed
3 cups vegetable stock
3 carrots, peeled and sliced
200 g broccoli florets
salt and pepper
lemon wedges to garnish

Heat the oil in a pot and sauté the onion and garlic until soft. Add the cumin, turmeric and cayenne pepper and stir-fry for 1 minute. Add the lentils and the stock, and stir for 1 minute to prevent the lentils from catching. Cover and simmer for 15 minutes. Finally, add the vegetables and cook until they are tender but firm. Season with the salt and pepper. Transfer to a serving dish, then garnish with the lemon wedges. Serve with rice. **SERVES 4–6**

GRILLED STUFFED PEPPERS WITH COUSCOUS AND PINE NUTS

Although this is an excellent side dish if served with kebabs, because it includes couscous, olives and pine nuts, it is easily a stand-alone meal.

1½ cups water

½ tsp salt

1 Tbsp olive oil

200 g couscous

¼ cup green or black pitted olives, chopped

½ cup pine nuts, toasted

1 carrot, peeled and grated

½ cup grated cheddar cheese

3 red peppers, halved lengthways

salt and pepper

Preheat the oven grill.
Boil the water in a pot with the salt and olive oil. Gently stir in the couscous, cover and cook for 3 minutes. Remove the pot from the heat and leave to stand for 5 minutes. Separate the grains with a fork, then add the olives, pine nuts, carrot and cheese. Season the peppers with salt and pepper and stuff them with the couscous mixture. Grill on the middle shelf of the oven for 10 minutes. **SERVES 4–6**

STUFFED BRINJALS WITH CABBAGE AND LENTILS

Brinjals are grown extensively throughout West Africa from where this dish the simpler version of this dish (without the feta and tofu) originates.

3 whole brinjals

4 Tbsp olive oil

1 onion, chopped

3 cloves garlic, crushed

1 tsp cumin seeds

150 g white cabbage, thinly sliced

1 cup red lentils, cooked

salt and pepper

100 g feta cheese, crumbled

100 g smoked tofu, crumbled

cayenne pepper

Preheat the oven to 180 °C. Wrap the brinjals in foil and roast for 20 minutes, or until just soft. Leave them to cool, then cut in half lengthways, scoop out the flesh but set aside both the flesh and the shells.
In a pot, heat the oil and sauté the onion and garlic until soft. Add the cumin seeds, cabbage and lentils and stir until heated through. Add the flesh from the brinjals, season with the salt and pepper, and stir to mix. Spoon the mixture back into the brinjal shells. Combine the feta and tofu and sprinkle over the top of the stuffed brinjals. Sprinkle with the cayenne pepper and grill in the oven until brown. **SERVES 4–6**

BAKED PHYLLO PIES WITH FETA, SPINACH AND PINE NUTS

Remember to inform your guests if you have used nuts in your cooking as some people are allergic to nuts, and that includes pine nuts. Roasting or toasting enhances the flavour of all nuts, and the pine nuts add to the protein value of this dish.

3 Tbsp olive oil
1 onion, finely chopped
100 g spinach, shredded, washed and dried
100 g feta cheese, crumbled
3 Tbsp green or black pitted and chopped olives
¼ cup pine nuts, toasted
2 medium baby marrows, grated
a pinch of nutmeg
salt and pepper
4 sheets phyllo pastry
a knob of melted butter

Preheat the oven to 160 °C. Grease a baking sheet. Heat the oil in a pot and sauté the onion until soft. Add the spinach and stir-fry until just soft. Remove from the heat and add the feta cheese, olives and pine nuts.

Squeeze out the moisture from the baby marrows by pressing them between the palms of your hands, then add to the spinach mixture along with the nutmeg. Season with the salt and pepper.

Brush each sheet of phyllo pastry with the melted butter. Cut the sheets into 8 squares measuring 6 x 6 cm. Spoon a tablespoon of spinach mixture onto each square and fold them in half to form triangles. Arrange the triangles onto the baking sheet, brush the tops with melted butter and bake for 15 minutes. Serve with a salad. **SERVES 4–6**

VEGETABLE FRITTERS WITH AVOCADO AND TOMATO SALSA

This dish could be served as a starter, as well as a main course.

2 potatoes, peeled and grated
2 large carrots, peeled and grated
2 baby marrows, washed and grated
1 onion, finely chopped
4 eggs, lightly beaten
6 Tbsp cake flour
salt and cayenne pepper
vegetable oil for frying

SALSA
3 ripe avocados, peeled and cubed
¼ cup drained and chopped sun-dried tomatoes
¼ cup chopped fresh coriander
¼ cup olive oil
2 Tbsp fresh lemon juice
1 Tbsp Tabasco®

First make the salsa by mixing all the ingredients together gently. In a bowl, mix the potatoes, carrots and baby marrows. Using the palms of your hands press the vegetables to squeeze out excess moisture, then drain. Stir in the onion, eggs, flour and salt and cayenne pepper. Heat the oil (about 3.5 cm deep) in a pan and drop in a tablespoon of the mixture and flatten with a fork to form a pattie. Fry for 3 minutes per side, until brown. Repeat with the remaining mixture.

Serve the fritters topped with the salsa. **SERVES 4–6**

DUNGU CURRIED VEGETABLES AND RICE

This dish comes from Dungu, which is a province in the Democratic Republic of the Congo.

2 Tbsp olive oil
1 onion, chopped
2 Tbsp medium curry powder
1 tsp ground cumin
1 tsp ground coriander
1 fresh green chilli, chopped
2 cloves garlic, crushed
1 large red pepper, cubed
1 large green pepper, cubed
1 large yellow pepper, cubed
3 carrots, peeled and sliced
200 g fresh green beans, halved
400 g tomatoes, sliced and fried
150 g frozen peas
½ cup water
salt and pepper

Heat the oil in a casserole dish and fry the onion until soft. Add the curry powder, cumin, coriander, chilli and garlic and fry for 3 minutes, then add the rest of the ingredients and simmer for 20 minutes.
Serve on a bed of rice. **SERVES 4–6**

BAKED MUSHROOMS WITH AVOCADO, ASPARAGUS AND CHEESE

This simple dish makes for a light but delicious lunch.

6 large black mushrooms
200 g green asparagus spears, cooked
2 avocados, mashed
juice of 1 lemon
½ tsp salt
a pinch of cayenne pepper
100 g cheddar cheese, grated

Preheat the grill.
Wipe the mushrooms with paper towel then arrange them on a baking tray. Place the asparagus on top of the mushrooms.
Grill for 3–5 minutes.
Combine the avocados, lemon juice, salt and cayenne pepper and spoon the mixture over the asparagus-topped mushrooms.
Sprinkle with the grated cheese and grill for another 3 minutes.
SERVES 4–6

Dungu curried vegetables and rice

VEGETABLES ON A BED OF COUSCOUS

*Although Mediterranean flavours dominate in this dish, this type
of meal has travelled south and is served throughout Africa.*

4 tsp olive oil
2 medium onions, sliced
2 cloves garlic, crushed
1 brinjal, cubed
2 baby marrows, sliced
1 red pepper, cubed
1 x 410 g can peeled tomatoes
½ tsp dried basil
½ tsp dried origanum
a pinch of sugar
salt and pepper
2 cups couscous, prepared according to packet instructions

Heat 2 teaspoons of the oil and sauté the onions and garlic until
soft. Add the remaining oil and sauté the brinjal for 5 minutes.
Add the baby marrows, red pepper, tomatoes, basil, origanum,
sugar, and salt and pepper, then simmer slowly for 5 minutes.
Serve on a bed of couscous. **SERVES 4–6**

GRILLED VEGETABLES AND MEALIEPAP STACK

*Mealiepap is number one on the list of popular African foods and
is traditionally eaten by hand straight from the pot and dipped
in a tasty sauce.*

MEALIEPAP
4 cups water
1 tsp salt
50 g butter
2 cups mealie meal

VEGETABLES
2 onions, cut into wedges
1 brinjal, cubed
2 red peppers, cubed
2 green peppers, cubed
6 tomatoes, peeled and quartered
4 Tbsp shredded basil
4 Tbsp olive oil
salt and pepper

Bring the water to the boil and add the salt, butter and mealie
meal while stirring continuously. Cook, covered, over a low heat
for 20 minutes. Spread out in a buttered, flat dish so that the
mealiepap is about 2 cm thick.
Preheat the grill. In a bowl, toss together the onions, brinjal,
red peppers, green peppers, tomatoes, basil, olive oil, and salt
and pepper. Transfer the vegetables to a baking dish. Grill for
15–20 minutes, or until cooked.
Cut the mealiepap into wedges, pile with the vegetables,
then add more mealiepap on top. Repeat with another layer
of vegetables and mealiepap. **SERVES 4–6**

Grilled vegetables and mealiepap stack

CHICKPEA, BRINJAL AND MUSHROOM TAGINE

This is a typical Moroccan vegetarian tagine. Almonds, chickpeas, olives, coriander, cumin, cinnamon and turmeric are all key ingredients in Moroccan cuisine.

3 Tbsp vegetable oil
2 onions, chopped
2 cloves garlic, crushed
1 Tbsp ground cumin
½ tsp cayenne pepper
1 Tbsp ground coriander
1 tsp ground cinnamon
1 tsp turmeric
1 x 410 g can peeled tomatoes
2 medium brinjals, cubed
1 x 410 g can chickpeas, drained
200 g button mushrooms, halved
1 cup vegetable stock
3 Tbsp chopped fresh coriander
salt and pepper
50 g toasted almonds

In a large pot, heat the oil and sauté the onions until soft. Add the garlic and spices and fry for 2 minutes. Pour in the tomatoes and cook for 10 minutes, then add the brinjals, chickpeas, mushrooms, stock and coriander and simmer, covered, for 15 minutes, or until the brinjals are cooked. Season with the salt and pepper. Spoon into a serving dish and sprinkle with the almonds. Serve with rice or couscous **SERVES 4–6**

BRINJAL STEW WITH POTATOES

If this dish is to be served to vegans (strict vegetarians), substitute the chicken stock with vegetable stock.

2 Tbsp vegetable oil
2 onions, roughly chopped
1 clove garlic, crushed
5 brinjals, cubed
5 potatoes, peeled and cubed
5 tomatoes, peeled and chopped
2 cups chicken stock
salt and pepper

In a large pot, heat the oil and sauté the onions for 5 minutes. Add the garlic and the rest of the vegetables. Pour in the stock.

Adjust the seasoning to taste with the salt and pepper and simmer gently for 15–20 minutes.

Serve with rice. **SERVES 4–6**

Chickpea, brinjal and mushroom tagine

SWEET POTATOES AND VEGETABLE BAKE

Using sweet potatoes instead of ordinary potatoes, and the addition of butternut and baby marrows, creates a somewhat different version of the usual potato bake.

6 medium sweet potatoes, unpeeled and sliced
3 onions, thinly sliced
3 cloves garlic, crushed
2 cups diced butternut
3 medium baby marrows, sliced
3 Tbsp chopped fresh coriander
1½ cups fresh cream
¼ cup olive oil
salt and pepper
100 g cheddar cheese, grated
½ cup stale breadcrumbs or cornflake crumbs

Preheat the oven to 180 °C. Grease a deep ovenproof dish. In a large bowl, combine the sweet potatoes, onions, garlic, butternut, baby marrows, coriander, cream, olive oil, and salt and pepper. Toss thoroughly and spoon into the prepared dish. Mix together the cheese and breadcrumbs and sprinkle on top. Cover with foil and bake for 30 minutes, then uncover and bake until brown. **SERVES 4–6**

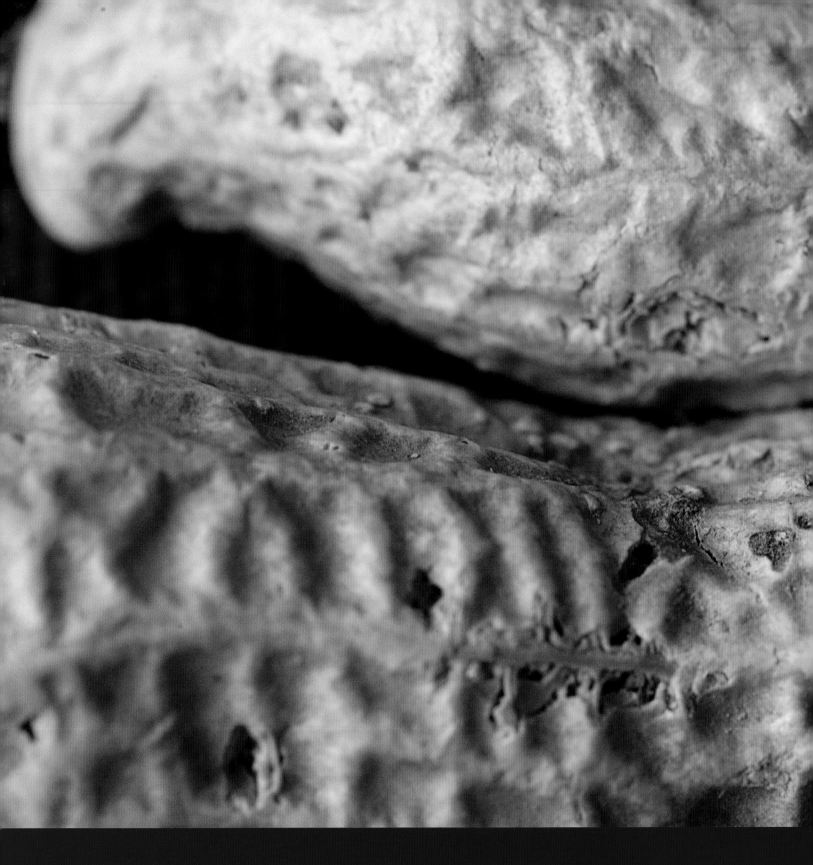

SIDE DISHES AND

ACCOMPANIMENTS

PILAU RICE

The term 'pilau' refers to rice that has been browned in oil and then simmered in a spicy liquid.

2 Tbsp olive oil
2 onions, chopped
2 cups uncooked white rice
2 cloves garlic, crushed
½ tsp ground cumin
1 Tbsp tomato paste
8 cups water
salt and pepper
¾ cup cashew nuts

Heat the oil in a saucepan and sauté the onions for 3 minutes. Stir in the rice, garlic, cumin and tomato paste, then add the water, and salt and pepper. Cook for 15 minutes, or until the water has evaporated, and stir in the cashew nuts just before serving. **SERVES 4–6**

SAVOURY RICE

In Sanskrit basmati means 'the flavoured one', which is no surprise as this variety of long-grained rice is extremely tasty and aromatic.

2 Tbsp vegetable oil
1 Tbsp butter
1 onion, finely chopped
2 cups white basmati rice
1 tsp caraway seeds
1 carrot, peeled and diced
100 g brown mushrooms, sliced
6 cups water
salt and pepper to taste
2 baby marrows, diced
100 g shelled peas

Heat the oil and butter in a pot and sauté the onion until soft. Add the rice and caraway seeds and fry for 2 minutes before adding the carrot and mushrooms. Stir for another 2 minutes, then pour in the water. Season with the salt and pepper and cook for 10 minutes. Finally, add the baby marrows and peas, and cook for a further 5 minutes. Fluff the rice up with a fork, and serve with stews or curries. **SERVES 4–6**

Pilau rice

GREEN BEAN AND TOMATO SALAD

Cherry tomatoes are very attractive in this salad, but if you don't have any to hand, use sliced standard-size tomatoes instead.

500 g green beans, topped, tailed and halved
2 small punnets ripe cherry tomatoes, halved
salt and pepper

DRESSING
5 Tbsp olive oil
2 Tbsp white vinegar

Steam the green beans until they are tender but still crunchy. Arrange the beans and tomatoes in salad bowl. Mix the olive oil and vinegar together and pour over the beans and tomatoes. Season to taste with the salt and pepper. **SERVES 4–6**

NORTH AFRICAN COUSCOUS SALAD

Although the North African city of Carthage had been destroyed in 146 BCE, the Romans re-established it 100 years later and decided that it should be a supplier of wheat to their empire. And so this once agriculturally diverse area became a one-crop province, supplying two-thirds of Rome's wheat needs. The result was that the Carthaginian diet was dominated by wheat and its by-products, including semolina. Berbers adapted semolina into couscous and spread its popularity throughout North Africa. Couscous refers to both the dry, uncooked semolina pellets as well as to the dish of light and fluffy steamed grains.

1 cup uncooked couscous
1 cup water
1 small onion, chopped
¼ English cucumber, finely chopped
1 firm tomato, chopped
½ bunch fresh mint, chopped
½ bunch fresh parsley, chopped
8 pitted black olives, chopped
salt and pepper
1 lettuce, leaves separated

DRESSING
¼ cup olive oil
2 Tbsp lemon juice
2 Tbsp brown vinegar
salt and pepper

To make the dressing, combine all the ingredients.
In a saucepan, combine the couscous and water. Cover and bring to the boil for 3 minutes, or until all the water is absorbed. Leave to cool. Mix in the onion, cucumber, tomato, mint, parsley and olives, as well as the dressing. Stir with a fork to separate the grains. Season with the salt and pepper. If dry, add extra olive oil and lemon juice. Serve on a bed of lettuce. **SERVES 4–6**

MALAWI'S FAVOURITE CABBAGE SALAD

This is Malawi's more interesting version of the common coleslaw. The dressing is the secret!

½ medium green cabbage, finely shredded
2 carrots, peeled and grated
1 onion, chopped
1 yellow pepper, finely julienned
1 red pepper, finely julienned
¼ cup unsalted peanuts
1½ cups finely shredded red cabbage

DRESSING
1 tsp Dijon mustard
4 Tbsp olive oil
150 ml vinegar
150 ml vegetable oil
⅓ cup brown sugar

To make the dressing, stir all the ingredients together until the sugar has dissolved.
Toss all the salad ingredients together in a salad bowl, pour over the dressing and serve immediately. **SERVES 4–6**

CUCUMBER AND BABY MARROW SALAD

This salad is particularly attractive as the thin slices of cucumber and baby marrow create a ribbon effect. Use a potato peeler to achieve these ultra-thin slices.

3 English cucumbers, thinly sliced lengthways
10 baby marrows, thinly sliced lengthways
¼ cup olive oil
1 cup roasted cashew nuts

DRESSING
¼ cup olive oil
3 Tbsp white vinegar
1 tsp wholegrain mustard
1 tsp honey
1 Tbsp chopped fresh coriander

Place the cucumber slices in a bowl. Heat a cast-iron griddle. Toss the baby marrows with the olive oil and grill for 1 minute on each side. Add to the cucumber and mix in the cashew nuts. Mix the dressing ingredients together and pour over the cucumber and baby marrows. Toss gently and serve at once. **SERVES 4–6**

COCONUT RICE

*If you add coconut milk to ordinary white rice it makes a
wonderful accompaniment to any curry dish.*

2 x 400 ml cans coconut milk
1 cup water
3 Tbsp olive oil
1 tsp salt
2 cups uncooked white rice

In a pot, heat the coconut milk, water, olive oil and salt. Stir in the
rice to ensure that it does not stick together. Cook, uncovered, for
1 minute then cover and simmer for 15 minutes. Fluff up the rice
with a fork before serving. **SERVES 4–6**

RICE SALAD

A rice salad is a bright, cheerful accompaniment to braai dishes.

salt
6 cups water
2 cups uncooked white rice
1 cup seedless raisins
1 cup cooked green beans, cut into 1 cm lengths
¼ cup pitted olives
½ cup cubed cheddar cheese
4 spring onions, chopped
½ red pepper, chopped
1 tsp chopped fresh parsley
salt and pepper
cos lettuce for serving (optional)

DRESSING
160 ml lemon juice
160 ml olive oil
½ tsp wholegrain mustard
¼ tsp sugar
¼ tsp salt

Salt the water and bring it to the boil. Add the rice and raisins
and simmer for 20 minutes. Fluff up the rice with a fork to
separate the grains, then leave to cool before stirring in the
remaining ingredients, except the cos lettuce (if using).
To make the dressing, combine all the ingredients and drizzle
over the rice.
Serve on a bed of cos lettuce if you like. **SERVES 4–6**

Rice salad

THREE-BEAN SALAD WITH OLIVES

The only skill this salad requires is knowing how to use a can opener. The addition of a red onion and black olives gives it a special touch.

1 x 400 g can red beans, drained and rinsed
1 x 400 g can butter beans, drained and rinsed
1 x 400 g white beans, drained and rinsed
1 red onion, thinly sliced
12 pitted black olives
2 Tbsp chopped fresh parsley

DRESSING
¼ cup olive oil
3 Tbsp red or white vinegar
2 cloves garlic, crushed
1 Tbsp lemon juice
1 tsp brown sugar
1 tsp salt
freshly ground black pepper

Mix all the ingredients together in a salad bowl.
To make the dressing, whisk together the ingredients and pour over the bean mixture. Mix gently so as not to break the beans. Leave to stand for 1 hour before serving, for the flavour to develop. **SERVES 4–6**

RICE AND SWEETCORN SALAD

This simple salad can be made in advance for greater convenience, but if so, remember to keep it refrigerated and bring back to room temperature before serving.

2 cups water
2 cups uncooked white rice (preferably basmati)
¼ cup shelled peas
2 carrots, peeled and grated
2 cups cooked sweetcorn
lettuce leaves for serving

DRESSING
5 Tbsp olive oil
3 Tbsp red wine vinegar
salt and freshly ground pepper

Bring the water to the boil in a pot, then add the rice and cook, covered, for 10 minutes. Add the peas and cook for a further 5 minutes. Remove the pot from the heat and add the grated carrots and sweetcorn. Mix with a fork.
To make the dressing, mix all the ingredients together and drizzle over the rice.
Serve over a lettuce leaf on each plate. **SERVES 4–6**

Three-bean salad with olives

BRINJAL SALAD

Grilling the brinjals releases a smoky flavour that is enhanced by the addition of spices.

4 large brinjals, cubed
4 Tbsp sea salt
olive oil
1 cup cherry tomatoes, halved
1 red onion, finely chopped
1 Tbsp capers
ciabatta bread for serving
Greek yoghurt for serving
cayenne pepper

DRESSING
¼ cup olive oil
3 Tbsp lemon juice
3 cloves garlic, crushed
¼ tsp paprika
2 Tbsp chopped fresh coriander
a pinch of sugar
salt and pepper

Sprinkle the brinjals with the sea salt in a colander, then leave to stand for 30–60 minutes. Rinse the brinjals and pat dry. Transfer them to a roasting pan and drizzle with a little olive oil then toss. Ensure that they're lying in a single layer then place them under the grill until soft, but still firm. Transfer the brinjals to a bowl and add the tomatoes, onion and capers. Mix all the dressing ingredients together and pour over the brinjal salad. Toss gently. Serve on thick slices of bread topped with 1 tablespoon of yoghurt each. Sprinkle with the cayenne pepper and serve immediately. **SERVES 4–6**

CHICKPEA AND LENTIL SALAD

Both chickpeas and lentils are rich in protein. Lentils may vary in colour from yellow and red-orange to green, brown and black.

2 Tbsp olive oil
1 onion, chopped
½ tsp ground ginger
1 tsp ground cumin
1 fresh green chilli, finely chopped
200 g red lentils
1 x 400 g can chickpeas, drained
salt and pepper
1 cos lettuce for serving

DRESSING
6 Tbsp olive oil
6 Tbsp lemon juice
1 Tbsp wine vinegar
3 Tbsp chopped fresh parsley
salt and pepper

Heat the oil in a pot and sauté the onion until soft. Add the ginger, cumin, chilli and lentils. Stir thoroughly and pour in sufficient water just to cover the lentils, then simmer for 10 minutes or until all the water has been absorbed. Stir in the chickpeas and season to taste with the salt and pepper. Whisk together the dressing ingredients and pour over the chickpeas and lentils. Toss gently.
Serve on a bed of lettuce. **SERVES 4–6**

CHICKPEA SALAD
WITH BUTTERMILK DRESSING

Chickpeas with their high nutritional values are extensively cultivated in developing countries, particularly Ethiopia, Tanzania, Sudan and Kenya.

1 lettuce
1 x 400 g can chickpeas, drained
3 carrots, peeled and grated
6 cherry tomatoes
1 x 400 g can sweetcorn, drained
2 Tbsp sesame seeds

DRESSING

150 ml buttermilk
4 tsp chopped fresh parsley
4 tsp wholegrain mustard
1 tsp brown sugar

To make the dressing, mix all the ingredients together well. Separate the lettuce leaves without breaking them and arrange them in a serving dish. Toss the rest of the salad ingredients with the salad dressing. Spoon all on top of the lettuce leaves and serve immediately. **SERVES 4–6**

MEALIEPAP WITH ONION
AND TOMATO SAUCE

Many traditional African dishes include pap. This may take the form of a smooth maize meal porridge or a crumbly phutu pap. Because pap can be dry, it is generally served with a tomato and onion sauce.

6 cups water
1 tsp salt
3 cups mealie meal

SAUCE
4 Tbsp olive oil
3 onions, finely chopped
9 tomatoes, peeled and chopped
1 Tbsp tomato paste
1 beef stock cube
½ cup water
salt and pepper

In a pot, bring the water and salt to a boil and sprinkle in the mealie meal little by little, stirring with a wooden spoon. Reduce the heat until the mixture thickens, cover, and lower the heat. Cook over a low heat for 15 minutes.

To make the sauce, heat the oil in a medium pot and sauté the onions until soft. Add the tomatoes and tomato paste and stir over medium heat until the tomatoes are very soft. Stir in the beef stock and water until the cube has dissolved. Simmer for 15 minutes then season with the salt and pepper. (Don't forget that the beef stock is very salty.)

To serve, spoon the mealiepap onto plates and ladle over the sauce. **SERVES 4–6**

SEASONAL VEGETABLES WITH PEANUTS

4 Tbsp olive oil
1 onion, chopped
1 tsp ground cumin
½ tsp chilli powder
3 tomatoes, peeled and chopped
1 cup raw peanuts
1 red pepper, diced
1 yellow pepper, diced
½ cup sweetcorn kernels
salt and pepper

Heat the oil in a pot and sauté the onion until soft. Add the cumin and chilli and stir for 2 minutes, then add the tomatoes and cook until they are soft. Finally, add the peanuts, peppers and sweetcorn and simmer gently for 20 minutes until the vegetables are cooked. Season with the salt and pepper. Serve with rice or mealiepap. **SERVES 4–6**

Seasonal vegetables with peanuts

BUTTERNUT FRITTERS

A fritter comprises any kind of food that is coated in batter and deep-fried. The soft texture of butternut, as well as its natural sweetness combined with cinnamon-sugar, makes it the ideal fritter ingredient. In South Africa fritters are usually served as an accompaniment to a roast.

3 cups cooked and mashed butternut
50 ml cake flour
1½ tsp baking powder
1 egg, lightly beaten
½ tsp sugar
a pinch of salt
a knob of butter
cinnamon-sugar (3 Tbsp sugar mixed with
1 tsp ground cinnamon)

In a mixing bowl, combine the butternut, cake flour, baking powder, egg, sugar and salt.
Heat the butter in a pan and drop in tablespoons of the mixture, frying both sides until brown. Sprinkle with the cinnamon-sugar.
SERVES 4–6

BAKED CABBAGE WITH BACON AND POTATO

If you double the ingredient quantities this can be served on its own as a main meal.

3 potatoes, peeled and quartered
1 small cabbage, shredded
3 Tbsp butter
500 g rindless bacon, chopped
3 onions, chopped
1 x 410 g can peeled tomatoes
salt and pepper
1 cup grated cheese
1 cup cornflake crumbs
2 Tbsp chopped fresh parsley

Boil the potatoes until soft, then drain. Add the cabbage and butter and mash with a fork.

Preheat the oven to 180 °C. Grease an ovenproof dish. Fry the bacon and onions until cooked, add the tomatoes and simmer for 5 minutes. Season with the salt and pepper. Combine with the cabbage mixture and adjust the seasoning if necessary. Turn the mixture into the prepared dish. Mix the cheese, cornflake crumbs and parsley and sprinkle on top. Bake for 30 minutes.

SERVES 4–6

FUFU

Fufu is a staple food in West and Central Africa. Although the basic ingredients for it are plantains and fermented cassava, unripe bananas and yams (or sweet potatoes) also work well – the variations change according to the region. This popular version from Central Africa is eaten with beef, chicken or venison stews.

4 large unripe bananas (or plantains), peeled and washed
400 g yams, peeled and washed, or fermented cassava
3 Tbsp melted butter
salt
a pinch of cayenne pepper

Slice the bananas and cut the yams into small chunks. Put them all into a large pot and add just enough water to cover. Cook for 20 minutes, or until tender. Drain the water and add the butter, salt and cayenne pepper. Blend in a food processor until smooth. Shape into small balls and serve with a beef stew. **SERVES 4–6**

Baked cabbage with bacon and potato

EGYPTIAN CABBAGE ROLLS

Egyptian cuisine shares many similarities with that of the Eastern Mediterranean. Stuffed cabbage leaves may be likened to the more famous dish using vine leaves. Egypt's fertile Nile Valley and Delta allows for the production of high-quality vegetable crops.

1 cabbage, leaves separated
3 Tbsp vegetable oil
500 g minced lamb
1 tomato, peeled and chopped
2 Tbsp fresh breadcrumbs
salt and pepper
200 g cheddar cheese, grated

TOMATO SAUCE
3 Tbsp olive oil
2 onions, chopped
2 cloves garlic, crushed
2 x 410 g cans peeled tomatoes
1 fresh green chilli, chopped
1 Tbsp chopped fresh parsley
8 basil leaves, chopped
18 pitted green or black olives
salt and pepper

Blanch the cabbage leaves in boiling water until just soft. Mix together the oil, mince, tomato, breadcrumbs and seasoning. Wrap 2 tablespoons of the mixture in each leaf, to form rolls. To make the sauce, heat the oil in a saucepan and sauté the onions and garlic until soft. Add the tomatoes, chilli, parsley and basil and cook for 30 minutes. Add the olives and season with the salt and pepper.
While the sauce is cooking, preheat the oven to 180 °C. Pour half the tomato sauce in an ovenproof dish and arrange the cabbage rolls in the sauce. Pour the rest of the sauce over the rolls, sprinkle with the cheese and bake for 40 minutes. **SERVES 4–6**

ROASTED ROSEMARY POTATOES

This simple, inexpensive dish is full of flavour and is suitable for vegans as well as those on a gluten-free diet.

12 medium potatoes, washed and dried
3–4 Tbsp olive oil
3 Tbsp fresh rosemary
sea salt and pepper

Preheat the oven to 200 °C. Grease a roasting pan. Prick the potato skins with a fork, then arrange the potatoes in the roasting pan. Drizzle with the olive oil and sprinkle over the rosemary. Season with the salt and pepper and bake for 40 minutes. Serve immediately. **SERVES 4–6**

Egyptian cabbage rolls

CHARMOULA POTATOES

Charmoula marinade is used extensively in Algerian, Moroccan and Tunisian cooking and is an all-purpose North African sauce. The charmoula mix is quite spicy and goes well with fish, grilled meat or roasted vegetables.

6–8 potatoes
4 Tbsp olive oil
sea salt and freshly ground black pepper

CHARMOULA
½ tsp cayenne pepper
2 tsp turmeric
2 tsp cumin seeds
½ tsp salt
¼ cup chopped fresh coriander
2 Tbsp chopped fresh parsley
3 Tbsp white vinegar
3 Tbsp olive oil

Preheat the oven to 200 °C.
In a bowl, toss the potatoes with the olive oil, sea salt and pepper. Arrange them in a single layer in a roasting pan and roast for 30 minutes, or until cooked.
Blend all the charmoula ingredients together and toss with the potatoes while still hot. **SERVES 4–6**

SWEET POTATO AND BUTTERNUT MASH

This lovely, sweetish and yellow-coloured mash makes a great change from the usual potato mash.

500 g sweet potatoes, peeled and cubed
500 g butternut, peeled and cubed
3 Tbsp butter
1 tsp brown sugar
½ tsp ground cinnamon
¼ cup milk
¼ tsp salt

Boil the sweet potatoes and butternut for 10–15 minutes, or until cooked. Drain the water thoroughly, then add the butter, sugar and cinnamon. Mash until smooth, gradually adding the milk. Season with the salt. **SERVES 4–6**

SWEET POTATO CHIPS

This is a variation on the usual potato chip theme. Sweet potatoes are vitamin rich, fat free and a good source of fibre. Baked and sprinkled lightly with sea salt, they make a tasty snack. Ensure that the oil is not too hot otherwise they will burn or appear to be ready before they are cooked through.

3 sweet potatoes, peeled
4 cups vegetable oil
sea salt

Slice the potatoes into very thin rounds, then wash and pat them dry. In a pot, heat the oil and deep-fry the potatoes in small batches at a time. Fry until golden brown, then remove and drain on paper towel to absorb the excess oil. Sprinkle with the salt. **SERVES 4–6**

Sweet potato chips

HARISSA HOT CHILLI PASTE

Harissa is often called 'the flavour of North Africa'. It is particularly associated with Tunisia and is presented as a fiery chilli sauce often used in vegetable and meat tagines. However, harissa is also enjoyed in Algeria and Morocco and may be served as an accompaniment to couscous. Remember that red chillies are much hotter than green ones.

150 g fresh red or green chillies, deseeded and finely chopped
2 cloves garlic, crushed
1 green pepper, grilled, skinned and chopped
1 red pepper, grilled, skinned and chopped
¼ cup olive oil
2 Tbsp finely chopped fresh coriander
1 Tbsp sesame seeds, toasted
1 Tbsp ground cumin
sea salt

Combine all the ingredients and leave to stand for at least 30 minutes before using, for the flavour to develop. Store in a steralised jar in the refrigerator. **SERVES 4–6**

GARLIC POTATOES

This is such a simple dish yet very tasty with the combination of garlic and fried onion.

4 potatoes, cut into 1-cm cubes
5 cloves garlic, crushed
50 ml olive oil
1 tsp sea salt
2 Tbsp butter
1 large onion, sliced

Fry the potatoes and garlic in the oil for 10 minutes, until golden brown (shaking the pan occasionally). Remove the potatoes from the pan and drain on paper towel to absorb any excess oil. Season with the salt and keep warm.
In a clean pan, melt the butter and fry the onion until soft, then add to the potatoes and mix well to combine. **SERVES 4–6**

Harissa hot chilli paste

HUMMUS

Hummus, the Arabic word for chickpea dates back 7 000 years to the ancient Egyptians. In Spain chickpeas are known as garbanzo beans and in Italy they are called cece beans. Tahini is a ground sesame seed paste.

400 g cooked chickpeas or 1 x 400 g can chickpeas, drained
4 Tbsp lemon juice
4 Tbsp tahini
4 Tbsp olive oil
1 clove garlic
½ tsp salt
olive oil for drizzling
cayenne pepper to taste

In a food processor, blend the chickpeas, lemon juice, tahini, olive oil, garlic and salt until smooth. Spoon into a bowl, drizzle with the olive oil and sprinkle with the cayenne pepper. **SERVES 4–6**

J'S SPICED FRUIT CHUTNEY

Chutney is a great accompaniment with many meals and is also a tasty ingredient for marinating and basting steak and meat dishes. Instead of using store-bought chutney, I decided to make my own – to have more control over the flavours. Because there are no preservatives in the chutney, store it in a sealed bottle and keep refrigerated for up to two weeks. But I don't think it will even last that long as you'll find excuses to enjoy it with everything!

300 g dried pears, chopped
300 g seedless raisins
300 g dried apricots, chopped
300 g pitted dates, chopped
300 g dried apple rings, chopped
4 cups water
300 ml white vinegar
200 g sugar
1 Tbsp chilli powder
1 tsp turmeric
1 tsp ground ginger
1 fresh green chilli

In a large bowl, soak all the dried fruit in the water and vinegar for 4 hours. Transfer to a large pot and add the remaining ingredients. Simmer over a low heat for 2 hours, stirring every 15 minutes, until thick. Discard the whole chilli after cooking. **SERVES 4–6**

J's spiced fruit chutney

PRESERVED LEMONS

A traditional accompaniment to Moroccan dishes, these lemons are pickled in salt, together with their own juice. It is important to remember that they need to be bottled for about three weeks before they are ready for use.

500 g lemons
4 cups water
300 g sugar
1 Tbsp lemon juice
4 bay leaves
1 tsp coriander seeds
1 fresh long red chilli, sliced

Sterilise a preserve jar with 1-litre capacity.
Wash the lemons and scrub them with a brush. Place them in a pot with the water, sugar, lemon juice and bay leaves, bring to the boil and simmer for 30 minutes. Once cooled, cut the lemons into quarters and remove the pips.
Heat the sterilised jar in hot water, then pack the lemons into it with the coriander seeds and chilli. Boil the syrup again then pour into the jar. Seal immediately.

BREADS

SOUTH AFRICAN HEALTH BREAD

Nutty wheat is a popular flour in South Africa. Comprising white bread flour and a percentage of digestive bran, it is rich in vitamins and minerals. However, it may be substituted with any other flour for this recipe. Poppy seeds are a good source of calcium while sunflower seeds are high in vitamin E.

600 g nutty wheat flour
1 x 10 g sachet instant yeast
4 tsp sesame seeds
4 tsp poppy seeds
2 Tbsp sunflower seeds
2 Tbsp vegetable oil
1¾ cups lukewarm water
1 Tbsp brown sugar
½ tsp salt

TOPPING
1 Tbsp raw oats
1 Tbsp sesame seeds

Grease a large loaf tin. Combine all the ingredients, except the topping, and spoon into the tin.
Mix the oats and sesame seeds together, and sprinkle over the dough. Leave to rise, covered, in a warm place for 1 hour.
Preheat the oven to 180 °C. Bake for 40 minutes.
MAKES 1 LARGE LOAF

BREAD WITH PUMPKIN AND SESAME SEEDS

Pumpkin, one of Africa's best-loved vegetables, via its seed is also a rich source of Omega-3 fatty acids, essential in any healthy diet. Sesame seeds are full of magnesium and calcium, so all in all, this is a very healthy bread. It is also delicious and can be served with any simple meal, or even on its own dipped in olive oil. It is claimed that the Mediterranean habit of dipping bread in olive oil began in North Africa and spread from there to Spain, Italy and Greece.

200 g brown bread flour
100 g semolina
½ cup vegetable oil
1 tsp salt
180 ml water
3 Tbsp sesame seeds
4 Tbsp pumpkin seeds
1 tsp brown sugar
2 tsp instant yeast

Grease a medium-sized loaf tin. Combine all the ingredients and spoon into the tin. Cover and leave to rise in a warm place for 40–60 minutes. You will know when it is ready when it has doubled in volume.
Preheat the oven to 180 °C. Bake for 40 minutes.
MAKES 1 MEDIUM LOAF

South African health bread (left), and
Bread with pumpkin and sesame seeds (right)

CHEESE AND CHIVES BREAD

Spread with butter, this delicious savoury bread is good enough on its own, or you could serve it with extra cheese.

500 g white bread flour
1 tsp salt
1 tsp sugar
1 x 10 g sachet instant yeast
6 Tbsp chopped fresh chives
100 g cheddar cheese, grated
50 g butter, softened
1½ cups warm milk

Grease a large loaf tin.
Sift the flour and salt into a large bowl. Add the sugar, yeast and chives. Stir thoroughly until well combined, then add three-quarters of the cheese and the remaining ingredients. Turn the dough out onto a floured surface and knead for 10 minutes. Transfer the dough to a bowl dusted with flour, cover and leave in a warm place for 1 hour. Knock the dough down and knead again. Place it in the prepared loaf tin and leave to rise again, until it doubles in size. Sprinkle the remaining cheese on top. Preheat the oven to 180 °C. Bake for 40 minutes.

MAKES 1 LARGE LOAF

RAISIN BREAD

This healthy bread, with its slightly sweetish taste, is the ideal accompaniment to serve with a simple breakfast.

2 cups nutty wheat flour
1 cup white bread flour
1 tsp salt
1 cup digestive bran
1 x 10 g sachet instant yeast
1½ cups seedless raisins
1½ cups warm milk
3 Tbsp honey
50 g butter, softened

Grease a large loaf tin.
In a bowl, sift together the nutty wheat flour, bread flour and salt, then add the bran, yeast and raisins. Combine the milk and honey, then add to the dry ingredients, along with the butter. Turn out onto a floured surface and knead lightly for 8 minutes. Place in a bowl and dust with flour, cover with a cloth and leave to rise for 1 hour. Knock the dough down and transfer to the prepared loaf tin. Cover and leave to rise for 30 minutes.
Preheat the oven to 180 °C. Bake for 40 minutes.
MAKES 1 LARGE LOAF

Cheese and chives bread

TRADITIONAL WHITE BREAD

Many people in Africa still prefer white bread to brown bread and with the aroma of this newly baked bread permeating the house, who can blame them? The recipe instructions are for two large loaves, but you could make one extra-large loaf if you prefer.

1 kg white bread flour or cake flour
1 Tbsp salt
1 Tbsp white sugar
1 x 10 g sachet instant yeast
400 ml warm milk
¾ cup warm water
70 g margarine or butter

Grease 2 large loaf tins.

In a bowl, sift together the flour and salt, then add the sugar and yeast. Combine the milk and water and mix in the margarine or butter. Pour this into the dry mixture and mix. Turn out onto a floured surface and knead the dough until smooth. Transfer the dough to a bowl, dust with flour, cover with a cloth and leave to rise in a warm place until it has doubled in volume. Knock the dough down and divide it between the prepared loaf tins. Leave to rise for 40 minutes.

Preheat the oven to 200 °C. Brush the tops of the dough with a little milk and bake for 40 minutes. **MAKES 2 LARGE LOAVES**

COUNTRY BREAD WITH OLIVE OIL

Baking bread with olive oil is typically North African. This style of bread has found its way south over the years.

500 g brown bread flour
100 g cake flour
1½ tsp salt
1 x 10 g sachet instant yeast
2 tsp brown sugar
180 ml warm milk
100 ml olive oil

Grease a baking tray with oil, then dust with a little flour.

Sift the bread flour, cake flour and salt into a large bowl, then mix in the yeast. Dissolve the sugar in the milk then stir in the olive oil. Pour the liquid mixture into the flour mixture and mix. Turn out onto a floured working surface and knead until smooth. Transfer the dough to a bowl, dust the top with flour, cover and leave to rise for 1 hour. Divide the dough in half and shape each into a round loaf.

Place the loaves onto the prepared baking tray and press them down slightly with the palm of your hand. Cut an 'X' into the tops and dust with flour. Leave to rise until they double in size.

Preheat the oven to 200 °C. Bake for 30 minutes.

MAKES 2 SMALL LOAVES

Traditional white bread

SPECIAL CORNMEAL BREAD

*Because mealie meal (corn or maize meal) is so nutritious and
a staple food in most African countries, cornmeal bread is very
common throughout the continent.*

150 g mealie meal
100 g white bread flour
2 tsp baking powder
¼ tsp bicarbonate of soda
1½ Tbsp brown sugar
¼ tsp salt
50 g butter, melted
1 egg, beaten
150 ml buttermilk
150 ml milk

Preheat the oven to 180 °C. Grease a medium-sized loaf tin.
In a bowl, combine the mealie meal, flour, baking powder,
bicarbonate of soda, sugar and salt.
In another bowl, lightly mix together the butter, egg, buttermilk
and milk. Fold this into the dry mixture and mix thoroughly. Spoon
into the prepared loaf tin and bake for 25–30 minutes.

MAKES 1 MEDIUM LOAF

EGYPTIAN BREAD WITH VEGETABLES AND NUTS

*In Egyptian cuisine, bread is part of most meals and in rural
homes a meal may offer little more than bread and beans.*

50 g butter
1 onion, chopped
½ red pepper, seeded and chopped
2 cloves garlic, crushed
200 g white bread flour
2 tsp instant yeast
1 tsp salt
2 Tbsp chopped cashew nuts
1 tsp chopped fresh herbs (e.g. parsley, basil)
2 Tbsp sunflower seeds
1 tsp sugar
½ cup water
1 egg, beaten
salt and pepper

Grease a medium-sized loaf tin.
In a pan, melt the butter and sauté the onion and red pepper for
2 minutes. Add the garlic and fry for another 2 minutes. Remove
from the heat and leave to cool.
Mix in the rest of the ingredients. If the mixture seems a bit dry,
add a little more water. Spoon into the loaf tin and leave to rest
for 1½ hours.
Preheat the oven to 180 °C. Bake for 30 minutes.

MAKES 1 MEDIUM LOAF

Egyptian bread with vegetables and nuts

OATS BREAD

Oats, a popular African grain, make for a great energy-boosting bread with a lovely nutty flavour. Simple to make, this loaf has a very high carbohydrate content.

150 g raw oats
1 tsp salt
100 g white bread flour
200 g wholewheat flour
320 ml water
1 tsp brown sugar
2 tsp instant yeast
2 Tbsp vegetable oil or olive oil
extra oats for sprinkling

Grease a large loaf tin.
In a bowl, mix all the ingredients (except the oats for sprinkling) together, then knead the dough until smooth. Transfer the dough directly to the prepared loaf tin, cover and leave to rise until approximately double in volume. Sprinkle with the extra oats.
Preheat the oven to 180 °C. Bake for 1–1½ hours.
MAKES 1 LARGE LOAF

Special cornmeal bread (front – page 166), and Oats bread (back)

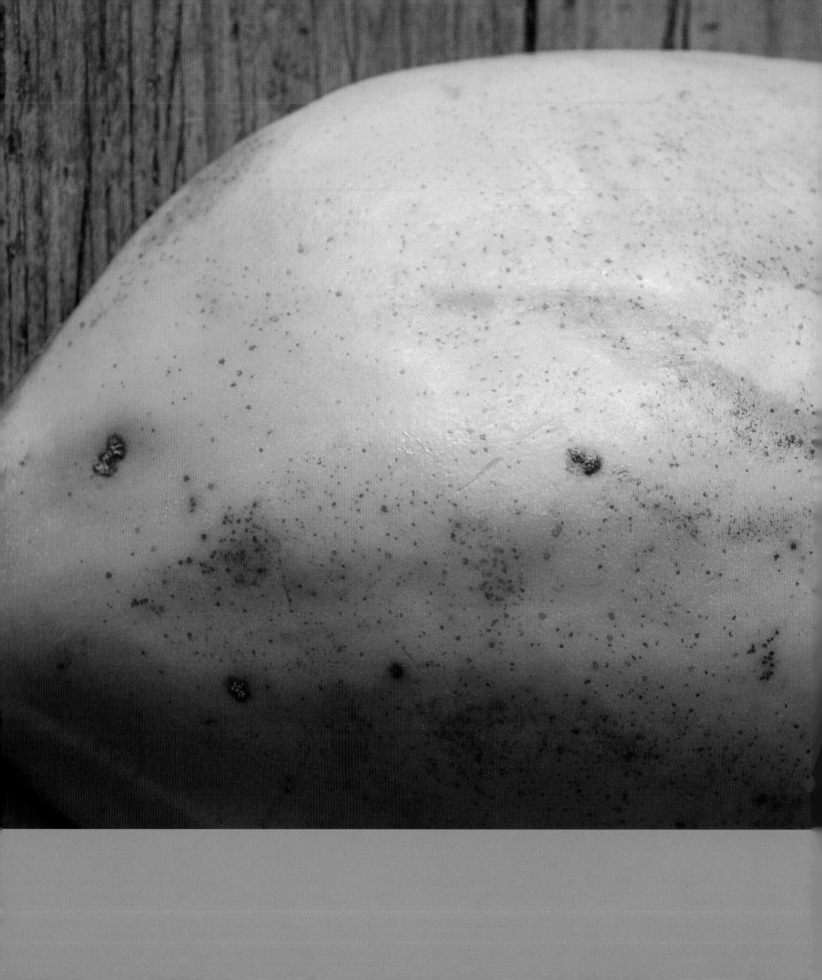

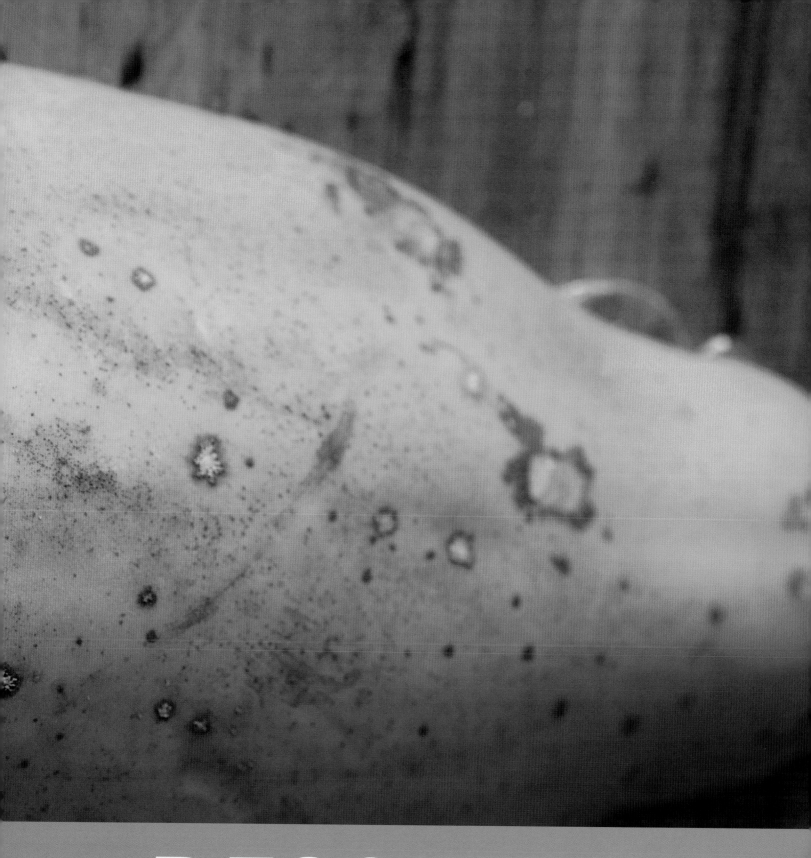

DESSERTS

BREAD AND BUTTER PUDDING

A good bread and butter pudding is just as popular in Africa as it is in the rest of the world. The secret to this version is the soaking of the sultanas in brandy beforehand! South Africa is home to delicious sultanas grown on the lower banks of the Orange River, as well as some award-winning brandies.

8 slices white bread, buttered and cut diagonally
50 g sultanas (soaked in 4 Tbsp brandy for 1 hour)
2 Tbsp candied peel
4 eggs
¾ cup milk
¾ cup fresh cream
100 g brown sugar
½ tsp ground cinnamon
a pinch of ground nutmeg

Preheat the oven to 160 °C. Grease an ovenproof dish suitable for the pudding.
Arrange the buttered bread in the prepared dish. Sprinkle over the sultanas and candied peel.
In a bowl, beat the eggs, milk, cream, sugar, cinnamon and nutmeg. Pour the mixture over the bread and leave to soak for 30 minutes, then bake for 30 minutes.
Serve with mango ice cream (see page 179) or whipped cream. **SERVES 4–6**

CARROT PUDDING

This traditional baked pudding is made with grated carrots, raisins, walnuts and spices. Combined with the sauce, it is moist and dense and quite irresistible.

SAUCE
2 cups water
150 ml sugar
2 Tbsp butter
2 tsp vanilla essence
3 Tbsp brandy

BATTER
100 g soft butter
1 cup castor sugar
2 eggs
2 cups grated carrots
1½ cups self-raising flour, sifted
grated rind of 1 lemon
1 tsp ground cinnamon
a pinch of salt

Preheat the oven to 180 °C. Grease a medium-sized ovenproof dish.
To make the sauce, bring the water, sugar and butter to the boil for 3 minutes. Remove from the heat and stir in the vanilla essence and brandy. Pour into the prepared dish.
For the batter, combine the butter and sugar until soft, then beat in the eggs, one at a time. Add the carrots, flour, lemon rind, cinnamon and salt, and mix well. Spoon the mixture over the sauce and bake for 40 minutes.
Serve with custard. **SERVES 4–6**

Carrot pudding

LEMON FRIANDS

These little French, almond-based tea cakes are light and spongy in texture. Lemons are an integral part of North African cuisine and it's probable that French colonials introduced this adaptation of the little cakes to that region of Africa.

170 g butter
1 cup ground almonds
grated rind of 1 lemon
1⅓ cups icing sugar, sifted
⅓ cup cake flour, sifted
5 egg whites

Preheat the oven to 180 °C. Grease a 12-cup muffin pan and dust with flour.

Melt the butter in a saucepan. In a large bowl, mix together the almonds, lemon rind, icing sugar and cake flour, then stir in the melted butter.

Beat the egg whites until stiff peaks form and gently fold into the butter mixture with a large metal spoon. Half fill each cup of the muffin pan with the batter and bake for 15 minutes.

SERVES 4–6

GRILLED FRUIT KHAPELA

This recipe is named in honour of Khapela, a friend of mine who is a very good chef. He says any seasonal fruit will work well in this pudding, which is the perfect ending to a heavy meal.

3 peaches, cubed
2 kiwi fruits, peeled and cubed
12 strawberries, hulled and halved
1 pineapple, peeled and cut into small chunks

TOPPING
1 cup milk
75 g sugar
25 g cake flour
1 cup fresh cream

Place all the fruit in an oven-to-table dish.

In a saucepan, heat the milk over medium heat. Meanwhile, in another bowl, mix together the sugar, flour and 5 tablespoons of the hot milk until the flour has dissolved. Add this flour mixture to the rest of the hot milk, stirring until it is thick, then leave to cool completely.

Beat the fresh cream until thick and fold into the milk custard, pour over the fruit and grill for 4 minutes or until light brown on top. **SERVES 4–6**

Lemon friands

BISCUITS PADANA

The almonds, pine nuts and pistachios in these Italian-origin 'biscuits' add a really interesting, but delicious flavour. 'Padana' refers to the Val Padana (Po Valley) in northern Italy. This is one of my own favourite desserts.

220 g cake flour
a pinch of salt
180 g castor sugar
185 g butter
2 eggs, beaten
¼ cup milk
60 g almonds, blanched and skinned
60 g pine nuts, toasted
60 g pistachio nuts

Preheat the oven to 180 °C. Grease a 20-cm diameter cake tin. In a bowl, sift together the flour and salt, stir in the sugar and mix in the butter until the mixture is uniform. Add the eggs (reserving 1 teaspoon for later use) and milk. Mix until the dough is smooth. Stir in the nuts until evenly distributed. Press the mixture into the prepared tin, smoothing the surface, then brush with the reserved egg. Lightly demarcate the serving wedges with a knife, but do not cut too deeply. Bake for 40 minutes. Slice immediately after it comes out of the oven. Serve warm or cold, with whipped cream. **SERVES 6**

Biscuits Padana

CITRUS-BANANA PANCAKES

Bananas add a real African touch to these pancakes, but any other fruit could be substituted.

120 g cake flour
¼ tsp baking powder
¼ tsp salt
2 eggs
2 Tbsp vegetable oil
2 Tbsp water
350 ml milk
cinnamon-sugar (1 Tbsp sugar and 1 tsp ground cinnamon)
   for sprinkling

FILLING
3 bananas, sliced
2 Tbsp lemon juice
2 Tbsp brown sugar

In a bowl, sift together the flour, baking powder and salt. Beat together the eggs, oil, water and milk, then mix with the dry ingredients.
Heat a small non-stick frying pan (or grease an ordinary pan with oil), pour in a thin layer of batter and cook for 1 minute on each side.
In a bowl, combine the fruit with the lemon juice and sugar. Spoon some of the fruit mixture into the middle of each pancake, fold in half, and then half again. Sprinkle the cinnamon-sugar over the top.
Serve with ice cream. **SERVES 4–6**

MIXED BERRY FRUIT TART

*Fruit, including berries, grows so plentifully throughout Africa that
it is automatically associated with the continent's cuisine. The
colours of these mixed berries make this a particularly attractive
dessert, but you could use any combination of berries of your
own choice.*

PASTRY
350 g self-raising flour
175 g butter, softened
100 g castor sugar
1 egg, lightly beaten
milk for brushing over

FILLING
170 g icing sugar
200 g red currants
200 g raspberries
100 g blueberries

In a bowl, sift the flour, then rub in the butter and castor sugar.
Add the beaten egg and knead the dough gently for 5 minutes on
a floured surface. Leave to chill for 1 hour.
Preheat the oven to 200 °C. Grease a 23-cm loose-bottomed,
fluted flan tin. Roll out two-thirds of the pastry on a floured
surface, and line the base and sides of the prepared tin.
In a bowl, sieve the icing sugar over the fruit and toss. Spoon the
fruit into the pastry case. Roll out the remaining pastry, cut into
strips and use to create a lattice pattern over the fruit, sealing the
edges with water. Brush the pastry with a little milk and bake for
30 minutes until golden. **SERVES 4–6**

COCONUT-BLUEBERRY PUDDING

*This easy-to-make and exotic-tasting light dessert is another
perfect choice to serve after a heavy meal.*

1 Tbsp gelatine powder
⅓ cup hot water
1 cup coconut milk
1 cup fresh cream
½ cup brown sugar
1 cup plain yoghurt
1 cup fresh, frozen or canned blueberries
6 small ramekins

Dissolve the gelatine in the hot water until the granules have
dissolved. In a saucepan, heat the coconut milk and cream until
hot. Remove from the heat, then stir in the sugar until dissolved.
Stir in the gelatine and yoghurt until well combined.
Divide the blueberries between the ramekins and pour over the
coconut mixture. Refrigerate for 3 hours until firm.
Turn out onto a serving platter or serve directly in the ramekins.
SERVES 6

CHOCOLATE BROWNIES WITH FUDGE SAUCE

Admittedly the combination of brownie and fudge sauce is very rich, but who can resist such brownies?

BROWNIES

150 g butter

170 g dark chocolate

170 g brown sugar

2 eggs

60 g cake flour

1 tsp baking powder

a pinch of salt

3 Tbsp cocoa powder, dissolved in 3 Tbsp warm water

150 g pecan nuts, roughly chopped

70 g chocolate, roughly chopped

1 Tbsp icing sugar, sifted

SAUCE

¼ cup water

¾ cup castor sugar

1½ cups fresh cream

Preheat the oven to 160 °C. Grease a shallow, square baking tray.

Melt the butter and dark chocolate in a double boiler. In a bowl, lightly beat the sugar and eggs. Sift in the flour, baking powder and salt, then stir in the cocoa, melted chocolate, pecan nuts and chopped chocolate. Spoon the mixture into the prepared tin and bake for 30–40 minutes. Leave to cool, then sprinkle over the icing sugar and cut into squares.

For the sauce, heat the water and sugar in a saucepan until the mixture turns light brown. Stir in the cream, remove from the heat, but keep stirring. Transfer the sauce to a serving bowl and serve with the brownies. **SERVES 4–6**

MANGO ICE CREAM WITH STRAWBERRY SAUCE

The name 'mango' is a corruption of the Portuguese name for the fruit 'manga'. Mango makes a particularly good ice cream while the strawberry sauce adds a further exotic touch to this dessert. If you have an ice cream machine, the texture will be smoother, but it is not essential.

ICE CREAM

2 cups fresh cream

1 cup milk

¼ cup castor sugar

6 egg yolks, lightly beaten

½ tsp vanilla essence

4 ripe mangos, peeled, stoned and puréed

SAUCE

100 g strawberries, washed, hulled and halved

1 Tbsp sugar

juice of 1 lemon

To make the ice cream, heat the cream and milk over a low heat until just warm. Stir in the sugar until dissolved. Gently whisk the eggs into the cream mixture with a balloon whisk until the custard thickens. Remove the pan from the heat, then stir in the vanilla essence and mango purée until thoroughly combined. Leave to cool, then pour into a plastic bowl. Place in the freezer for 30 minutes, stir to break up the ice crystals and freeze again for another 30 minutes. Repeat the process then freeze until firm. To make the sauce, simply blend all the ingredients until smooth and pass through a fine sieve. Pour the sauce into individual serving dishes with a scoop of ice cream on top. **SERVES 4–6**

CUSTARD WITH CINNAMON BANANAS

The brandy in this dessert transforms it from something simple into a grande finale to a meal.

6 cups prepared custard
3 Tbsp brandy
6 bananas, each sliced into 8 slices
ground cinnamon for sprinkling

In a bowl, stir the custard and brandy together, then pour half a cup of custard into each of 6 wine glasses. Place 4 banana slices on top of the custard and sprinkle with cinnamon. Pour another half a cup of custard over the bananas, followed by 4 more banana slices. Sprinkle with cinnamon. Chill for 1 hour before serving. **SERVES 6**

BAKED CHEESECAKE WITH CHOCOLATE CRUST

To soften cream cheese, leave it out of the refrigerator for 3 hours.

2 x packets Tennis® biscuits, finely crushed
200 g butter, melted
¼ cup cocoa powder, sifted
any sliced fruit to decorate

FILLING
500 g cream cheese, softened
¼ cup castor sugar
4 eggs, lightly beaten
½ cup fresh cream
½ cup plain yoghurt
1 Tbsp cornflour
grated rind of 1 lemon
1 Tbsp vanilla essence

Preheat the oven to 180 °C. Grease a 20-cm springform cake tin. Mix together the biscuits, butter and cocoa powder, then press onto the bottom and sides the prepared cake tin.
Beat the cream cheese and castor sugar until the sugar has dissolved. Mix together the remaining filling ingredients until soft and combine with the cream cheese. Pour into the biscuit shell. Bake for 45 minutes, or until the centre is firm. Leave to cool, turn out of the tin and decorate the top with the sliced fruit.
SERVES 8–12

Baked cheesecake with chocolate crust

PAPINO BOATS WITH MANDAZI AND CREAM TOPPING

Mandazi or maandazi *are also called* mahamri *or* mamri*. These East African fried breads are similar to doughnuts, but are not as sweet. They are particularly popular in the Swahili-speaking areas of Kenya and Tanzania and are enjoyed with tea or coffee, or even after the main course at lunch or dinner.*

3 papinos, halved, peeled and seeded
whipped cream for serving

MANDAZI
65 g cake flour
¼ tsp salt
50 g butter
150 ml water
2 eggs, beaten
2 cups vegetable oil

To make the mandazi, sift together the flour and salt in a bowl. In a saucepan, heat the butter and water over low heat until the butter melts. Increase the heat and bring to the boil, then add all the flour at once, stirring quickly. Reduce the heat and keep stirring until the mixture is smooth. Leave to cool, then beat in the eggs until the mixture is smooth.
Heat the oil in a pan. Drop teaspoonfuls of the batter into the oil and fry until golden brown.
Fill the papino boats with the mandazi and top with whipped cream. **SERVES 6**

FRUIT KEBABS DIPPED IN MELTED CHOCOLATE

The slightly tart taste of these exotic fruits is a wonderful foil for the dark chocolate.

4 kiwi fruits, peeled and quartered
12 strawberries, washed and hulled
1 pineapple, peeled and cubed
1 yellow melon, peeled, seeded and cubed
6 bamboo skewers
200 g dark chocolate

Line a dish with greaseproof paper.
Pat dry all the fruit, then thread onto the skewers. Place the kebabs in a flat dish.
Melt the chocolate in a double boiler and stir until smooth. Pour the melted chocolate gently over the kebabs, turning them so that the fruit is completely coated. Arrange the kebabs in the prepared dish and refrigerate for 1 hour until set.
Serve on a platter, or individually, with whipped cream or ice cream. **SERVES 4–6**

Papino boats with mandazi and cream topping

STRAWBERRY MOUSSE

Strawberry mousse makes a light dessert on its own, or it may be used as a topping for pastries, a garnish for cakes or a base for sliced fruit.

1 kg ripe strawberries, washed and hulled
¼ cup castor sugar
¼ cup orange juice
1 cup double-thick natural yoghurt, chilled
1 cup whipping cream, chilled
2 tsp vanilla essence
½ cup soft brown sugar

Purée a quarter of the strawberries in a blender and slice the remainder. Sprinkle castor sugar and orange juice over the sliced strawberries. Carefully fold the berry purée into the sliced strawberry mixture and spoon into individual glasses. Place the yoghurt in a bowl and whip the cream until stiff peaks form, then fold into the yoghurt. Stir in the vanilla essence and spoon over the strawberries in a thick layer. Sprinkle generously with brown sugar and refrigerate for 4 hours. **SERVES 4–6**

Milk tart

MILK TART

Also known as melktert *in Afrikaans, this is one of the most famous and best-loved of South African desserts.*

PASTRY
200 g cake flour
a pinch of salt
100 g butter, softened
3 Tbsp castor sugar
2 egg yolks
3 Tbsp water

FILLING
2 cups milk
80 g cornflour
60 g sugar
2 eggs, separated
20 g butter
1 tsp vanilla essence
ground cinnamon to sprinkle

In a bowl, sift the flour and salt, then rub in the butter and castor sugar until it resembles fine breadcrumbs. Beat the egg yolks and water, add to the flour mixture and knead gently for 5 minutes on a floured work surface. Refrigerate the dough for 30 minutes. Preheat the oven to 200 °C. Grease a 23-cm flat dish. Roll out the pastry and line the prepared dish. Prick the base with a fork and bake blind for 10 minutes.
For the filling, pour the milk into a saucepan and mix in the cornflour and sugar. Heat, stirring until smooth. Bring to the boil and keep stirring until the mixture thickens. Whisk in the egg yolks. Remove from the heat and add the butter and vanilla essence. Beat the egg whites until stiff peaks begin to form, then gently fold into the milk mixture. Pour the mixture into the pastry case until it is level with the top and bake for 25 minutes. Leave to cool, sprinkle with the cinnamon, then slice. **SERVES 8–12**

STRAWBERRY AND YOGHURT ICE CREAM

This is a refreshing ice cream, with a lovely soft texture and intense strawberry flavour.

200 g strawberries, hulled and sliced
2 cups plain yoghurt
¼ cup condensed milk
1 Tbsp fresh lemon juice
extra strawberries and a sprig of fresh mint to decorate

Blend the strawberries and yoghurt in a food processor until smooth. Add the condensed milk and lemon juice and blend for a further 5–10 seconds. Pour into a plastic bowl and freeze, beating every 40 minutes (about 3 times in all or until it hardens and is smooth). Before serving, remove it from the freezer to allow it to soften a little.
Scoop into glasses and decorate with strawberries and mint.

SERVES 4–6

MOROCCAN CINNAMON RICE PUDDING

Rice pudding is served in one guise or another all over the eastern Mediterranean. This Moroccan version is particularly delicious.

4 Tbsp butter
2 Tbsp brown sugar
1 Tbsp ground cinnamon
1 tsp cardamom seeds
3 cups cooked basmati rice
¼ cup honey
¾ cup plain yoghurt
150 g soft-eating dried apricots, chopped
100 g pecan nuts, chopped
mint leaves to decorate

In a pot, heat the butter, stir in the sugar, cinnamon and cardamom seeds, and fry for 3 minutes. Add the rice, then fry until it is heated and coated with the spices. Stir in the honey, yoghurt, apricots and pecan nuts.
Spoon into serving bowls and garnish with the mint leaves.

SERVES 4–6

Moroccan cinnamon rice pudding

GLOSSARY

Baby marrow (*Cucubita pepo*): also known as zuccini or courgette.

Braai: this South African word, of Afrikaans/Dutch origin, refers either to a social gathering to prepare meat by grilling it outdoors (in this instance, short for *braaivleis*), the main barbecue equipment, or to the act of grilling food over coals.

Brinjal (*Solanum melongena*): also known as eggplant or aubergine.

Cassava (*Manihot utilissima*): a tuberous root with dense, white flesh. It is usually peeled and boiled, and then grated. Be aware though, as bitter cassava is poisonous until it is cooked. Fermented cassava is usually left to soak in water for three days before use.

Charmoula: also spelt 'chermoula'; a spicy marinade or sauce of Moroccan origin. Typical ingredients may include lemon rind and juice, garlic, small red chillies, ground cumin, coriander (ground seeds and leaves), parsley, mint, basil, olive oil and salt.

Mealiepap: a corn or maize meal porridge that is the staple food of many African peoples, particularly those in South Africa.

Okra (*Abelmoschus esculentus*): tapered seed pods that have a glutinous texture when cooked and provide body to soups and stews. They are also a source of vitamins A and C, calcium and iron.

Plantain (*Musa paradisiaca*): a crop related to the sweet banana, but firmer and lower in sugar content. Plantains are starchy, have a neutral flavour and are generally steamed, boiled or fried. They are available from fresh produce markets.

Papino: this orange-coloured, subtropical fruit is a variant of the pawpaw (*Carica papaya*), but is usually smaller than pawpaw. Papinos are grown commercially in South Africa.

Samp: maize kernels that have been stamped and broken, but not ground as fine as mealie meal.

Tagine: see page 9.

Yam (*Dioscorea* spp.): a starchy, tuberous root cultivated in the world's tropical regions. The flesh is white, yellow, pink or purple and is covered with a light grey to dark brown skin that must be removed before cooking.

CONVERSION CHART

METRIC	US CUPS	IMPERIAL
1 ml	¼ tsp	–
2–3 ml	½ tsp	–
4 ml	¾ tsp	–
5 ml	1 tsp	3/16 fl oz
15 ml	1 Tbsp	½ fl oz
25 ml	–	1 fl oz
50 ml	–	2 fl oz
60 ml	4 Tbsp	2 fl oz
80 ml	⅓ cup	2¾ fl oz
125 ml	½ cup	4 fl oz
200 ml	¾ cup	7 fl oz
250 ml	1 cup	9 fl oz
25 g	–	1 oz
50 g	–	2 oz
75 g	–	3 oz
100 g	–	4 oz
150 g	–	5 oz
200 g	–	7 oz
250 g	–	9 oz
500 g	–	1 lb 2 oz
750 g	–	1 lb 10 oz
1 kg	–	2 lb 4 oz

OVEN TEMPERATURES

°C CELSIUS	°F FAHRENHEIT	GAS MARK
100 °C	200 °F	¼
110 °C	225 °F	¼
120 °C	250 °F	1
140 °C	275 °F	1
150 °C	300 °F	2
160 °C	325 °F	3
180 °C	350 °F	4
190 °C	375 °F	5
200 °C	400 °F	6
220 °C	425 °F	7
230 °C	450 °F	8
240 °C	475 °F	9

RECIPE INDEX